IT'S ABOUT TIME

IT'S ABOUT TIME

Jeanne E. Sherrow

Zondervan Books
**Zondervan Publishing House
Grand Rapids, Michigan**

IT'S ABOUT TIME
© 1984 by The Zondervan Corporation
1415 Lake Drive, S.E.
Grand Rapids, Michigan 49506

Library of Congress Cataloging in Publication Data
Sherrow, Jeanne E.
  It's about time.

  Bibliography: p. 125
   1. Church and leisure.   2. Christian Life—1960-
  3. Sherrow, Jeanne E.   I. Title.
  BV4597.55.S53   1983   261   83-19704
  ISBN 0-310-46991-0

Book Design: Martha Bentley
Copyeditor: Joan K. Ostling

Unless otherwise indicated, Scripture quotations are from The New International Version, © 1978 by New York International Bible Society.

All rights reserved. No part of this publication may be reproduced, stored in an electronic system, or transmitted in any form or by any means, electronic, mechanical, photocopy, recording or otherwise, without the prior permission of the copyright owner. Brief quotations may be used in literary reviews.

Printed in the United States of America

84 85 86 87 88 / 10 9 8 7 6 5 4 3 2 1

To all those with whom I've shared
  my leisure
    my life
      my Lord . . .

And especially to
  Jan
    Jeanette
      Darlene
        Dawn

Contents

Acknowledgments 8

Preface 9

Introduction 13

1. Hard Questions 17

2. "Define It—and Spell It" 27

3. "No, Thank You" 35

4. Salt Without Savor 47

5. All Costs, Any Cost 59

6. Notebooks, Card Files, and Manila Folders 71

7. "If Only I Had Enough" 81

8. "His Yoke Is Easy, His Burden Light" 93

9. A Unique Opportunity 102

10. Quantity Versus Quality 118

Notes 122

Suggested Reading 125

Acknowledgments

Two are better than one,
  because they have a good return for their work:
If one falls down,
  his friend can help him up.
But pity the man who falls
  and has no one to help him up!
                                    Ecclesiastes 4:9–10

I have been uniquely blessed in the writing of this book, for I have had not simply one good friend, but several upon whom I could rely in the day-to-day frustrations as a neophyte author. The following people were really quite indispensable to the completion of this book, and I am profoundly grateful.

Mother—who steadfastly prayed and patiently stood by.

Dawn Murry—who so effectively exercised her gifts of encouraging, helping, and serving.

Marcia Zabriskie—who read and evaluated each page, offering gentle—but firm—suggestions for improvement.

Ginny Holladay—who deciphered my writing style and typed the manuscript.

The Norwood women's prayer group—who prayed me into and through this awesome task.

Judi Greene—who did most of the library research.

My students and colleagues—who understood and left me alone.

Judith Markham—who invited me to write this book, encouraged me as I did so, and consistently provided whatever assistance I needed.

Sue Clapp, Jeanette Filbert, Catherine Hubbard, Phyllis Jensen, Pat Mills—my faithful prayer partners.

. . . and all the others who, as I wrote, joined in "prayer and petition, with thanksgiving, present(ing) . . . requests to God" (Philippians 4:6) on my behalf.

Preface

One of my favorite authors, A. W. Tozer, whose writings have borne considerable impact upon my life, wrote this in the preface of his book, *The Divine Conquest:*

> The only book that should ever be written is one that flows up from the heart, forced out by the inward pressure. When such a work has gestated within a man it is almost certain that it will be written. The man who is thus charged with a message will not be turned back by any blasé considerations. His book will be to him not only imperative, it will be inevitable.[1]

Without a doubt, such has been the case with this book. Its writing was inevitable, for its ideas have been smoldering within me for many years, awaiting ignition into something alive and aglow. Most of them I have shared privately in conversation with my students, my family, and my friends, and publicly in a variety of speaking situations; but the message with which I have been charged has been awaiting its fuller release.

I offer it now to you, but only after careful and prayerful consideration of its ideas, concepts, and questions. By no means would I indicate that I have come to definitive conclusions regarding these issues, but here provided for your consideration are concerns which the Lord has placed upon my heart. I am very much in the process of having them clarified and their impact fully felt in my own life.

It is my prayer that even as I have been challenged, convicted, and changed by the Lord in the writing of this book, that you also will experience His working in your life as you read it.

There is a time for everything,
  and a season for every activity under heaven:
  a time to be born and a time to die,
  a time to plant and a time to uproot,
  a time to kill and a time to heal,
  a time to tear down and a time to build,
  a time to weep and a time to laugh,
  a time to mourn and a time to dance,
  a time to scatter stones and a time to gather them,
  a time to embrace and a time to refrain,
  a time to search and a time to give up,
  a time to keep and a time to throw away,
  a time to tear and a time to mend,
  a time to be silent and a time to speak,
  a time to love and a time to hate,
 a time for war and a time for peace.

He has made everything beautiful in its time. He has also set eternity in the hearts of men; yet they cannot fathom what God has done from beginning to end.
Ecclesiastes 3:1–8, 11

Introduction

I could just hear your response as you picked up this book and examined the title—"That's one book I don't need—I *have* no leisure!" or "What does leisure have to do with Christianity?" or "What will they think of next to write books about?" or "Humph. Leisure. What leisure?" Or perhaps, "I've been thinking about that lately—my life does seem a little hectic these days."

How long has it been since you have . . .
- taken a quiet walk through the woods, pausing long enough on the trail to ponder the wonders about you?
- sat at water's edge and contemplated its depth, its beauty, its moods?
- spent the day with your son doing something he especially enjoys and thereby learning new dimensions of him?
- listened—*really* listened—to your spouse, or maybe even had an in-depth conversation about something other than work, the house, or the children?

When was the last time you . . .
> phoned a friend unexpectedly and said, "Let's go for a walk; it's been a long time since we've had a good chat"?
> spontaneously organized a group for an evening of games and laughter and *fun?*
> read a good book that did something other than entertain you?

Whatever your response to the title and however you might answer the above questions, thanks for joining me in the consideration of how leisure fits into the Christian life. From my perspective, the phenomenon of leisure, its impact upon our society as a whole and upon the quality of our lives individually and collectively, is one of the major areas of concern in contemporary society. It is time that Christians led the way in making some positive contributions—making waves instead of riding them. It is simply not acceptable that we mirror society as it is, living our lives essentially without difference from our non-Christian counterparts. Somehow we must respond to this admonition from the Word:

> *Be very careful, then, how you live—not as unwise but as wise, making the most of every opportunity, because the days are evil.*
> Ephesians 5:15–16

Or as Phillips paraphrased the passage:

> *Live life, then, with a due sense of responsibility, not as men who do not know the meaning and purpose of life but as those who do. Make the best use of your time, despite all the difficulties of these days.*
> Ephesians 5:15–16

What is your response? Is it that
—we are living in a society such as never before existed, with technological advances thrusting us into new

decision-making arenas—especially the arena of critical ethical decisions?

—our children are facing peer pressure unequalled in any other generation and cannot be expected to withstand the pressure to conform, regardless of the standard?

—we must not be *too* different or we will lose our "witness"?

—Scripture, although it is "God-breathed and is useful for teaching, rebuking, correcting and training in righteousness" (2 Timothy 3:16) was, after all, written in a time when life was not so complex, when things were black and white, when people still believed in absolutes?

What is your *response?*

Without doubt these are difficult days in which to maintain a Christian lifestyle. Perhaps it would be even more accurate to say that these are days in which it is difficult to *identify* a Christian lifestyle. But because it is difficult, do we ignore our responsibility? If, indeed, we know the meaning and purpose of life, we *must* live our lives with a difference—even a radical difference. The alternative, of course, is to admit that we do *not* know the real meaning of life, and to continue on as we are.

The question becomes, then, do we want to make a difference in the world? Do we want the power of God to alter

> our thinking?
>> our relationships?
>>> our conversation?

Do we want to be under the control of the Holy Spirit
> in the use of our time?
>> in our day-to-day living?
>>> in our *lives?*

Or do we desire only the comfort of our faith, the security of knowing
> that we are His children?
>> that we can be confident of His faithfulness to us?
>>> that He will work together all things for our good?

If I weren't convinced that many of us *do* want to allow God to make a difference in our lives and in the world around us, I don't suppose I would have undertaken this endeavor. It is my belief that many of us as Christians simply haven't given much thought to the tremendously important, and frequently misunderstood, concept of leisure. With some insight into the importance of leisure in our lives and its effect upon society, perhaps we will endeavor to make some changes. This, at least, is my prayer.

1 | Hard Questions

The wonders of our age of technology never cease to amaze me! We are badgered, billed, and bullied by the wondrously omnipotent computer;
> hassled, harried, and helpless when faced with the complexities of the latest labor-saving device;
>> concerned, confused, and nearly consumed by the moral dilemmas inherent in rapid technological advances.

Indeed, unbelievable technological advances have been made in our society. Have you ever stopped to consider the tremendous implications of these in our individual lives? Many of the issues resulting from this Technological Age directly affect us; yet, as an extremely strategic sub-culture of our nation, we as Christians have buried our heads in the sand and pretended they do not and will not affect us. Further, we have failed to accept the challenge of turning the tide in basic moral and life issues and we acquiesce as if we were powerless to do something about them.

We are witnessing a cultural revolution, and we are, ourselves, by our passive compliance, engaging in it. Technology may be morally neutral of itself, but the issues Christians must address center on technological *capabilities*.

We now have in our possession the ability to do almost anything (and we do), but we make our decisions with little regard for the consequences. Science has enabled us to yield control over such basics as life and death, and we assume that because we *can* do so, we *may* do so. For example, a June 18, 1981, news story told of doctors at Mount Sinai School of Medicine in New York, who "punctured the heart of an abnormal fetus to destroy it in the womb while leaving its normal twin to survive and be born more than four months later as a healthy baby."[1] The killing (and I use that term advisedly) took place after the forty-year-old childless woman had undergone amniocentesis in the seventeenth week of her pregnancy, revealing she would give birth to twin boys—one normal and one afflicted with Down's syndrome. The woman said she would abort both fetuses, if necessary, rather than rear a retarded child. What would you have done, and what would be your rationale?

Life is cheap; technological knowledge without a godly perspective has seen to that. We are no longer acquainted with absolutes upon which we can build our lives; we have entered the era of a value system of no values (see Judges 21:25). As a result, we watch our families disintegrate and somehow manage to fool ourselves into thinking it is inevitable in Twentieth Century America. Divorce rates climb and the body of Christ contributes to the ascent. We become immune to the violence and crime around us and excuse our own children involved in alcohol and drug abuse, as well as promiscuous sexual activity.

Is it as upsetting to you as it is to me that of the 21,000,000 young people between the ages of 15 and 19, more than one-half have engaged in sexual activity outside of marriage? How do you respond to the fact that more than 1,000,000 teens become pregnant each year and 400,000 of these pregnancies are terminated by abortion? If this trend continues, of the girls who were 14 years old in 1980, more than 4 in 10 will be pregnant before reaching the age of 20; more than 1 in 5 will have given birth, and more than 1 in 7 will have had an abortion.[2] Where is the child you love represented in these statistics? Or do you honestly think that Christians are exempt from such things?

Or does nothing phase us any more? Have we been lulled into passivity and permissiveness?

Technology has improved our existence by making it easier, but what of the quality of our lives? What of our integrity as human beings, created in God's image? Life may be easier, but it surely isn't more simple—nor does it give much evidence of being better! Charles Brightbill, an eminent philosopher and writer in the field of leisure studies, seems something of a prophet now as we read his words penned in 1960, "The machine displaces toil, but it also frequently removes the sense of responsibility and conscience. Machines tell us 'how little' or 'how much' but not what is 'good' or 'bad.' "[3]

Another of the results of the Technological Age is the increased productivity which has led to our current malaise of affluence. (If you are wondering why I term it thus, I refer you to chapter 7). Despite economic recessions, we are nonetheless enjoying the abundance of material means as never before in our history. Whatever the economic difficulty individuals and families seem to be having in maintaining their lives (or is it their lifestyles?), there appears to be little significant effect upon consumption, especially the consumption of pleasure goods. We live in an age of entitlement, an era that stresses ownership and immediate gratification.

Not long ago I attended a regional camping and outdoor

show held in a nearby city. Expecting to find low attendance and discouragement on the part of the dealers attempting to sell their expensive (at least $35,000 seems expensive to me) motor homes, travel trailers and other recreational vehicles, I was surprised by the attendance and sales figures given me by the host committee. By the end of the second day, attendance had increased 43 percent over the previous year's attendance total. In addition, I was informed that the dealers were extremely happy with sales, one having sold two motor homes the day of my visit and another, two the day before. This, of course, was in addition to the impressive number of smaller RVs and accompanying paraphernalia purchased. In answer to my query as to how this could be so, given the current economic slump, my host explained that ten-year financing is now obtainable, and added, "You know the generation we're appealing to now; they're willing to buy anything as long as they can finance it."

He's right, you know. This is the age in which we find ourselves. We are so accustomed to having what we want, when we want it, that to wait is unthinkable. It is even unimaginable to forego pleasure items for day-to-day needs. Affluence has bred a generation of consumers—of things as well as experiences. It has given birth to the idea that we are *entitled* to *anything* we want to purchase, though it may take us years to complete the payments. We think nothing of high interest payments on items we *want*. Indeed the slogan encouraging us to buy now and pay later has become the American Way. Once again, the Word provides a very practical admonition:

> *As goods increase,*
> *so do those who consume them.*
> *And what benefit are they to the owner*
> *except to feast his eyes on them?*
> Ecclesiastes 5:11

21 / *Hard Questions*

Although for some it may be a bit unsettling, and we may wish it were otherwise, another of the ensuing realities of technology and automation is the new era of leisure. Some may want to dispute this, but many firms now operate on a four-day week; the average worker receives a number of holidays in addition to his annual vacation period (in one state, these add up to two full weeks of additional vacation time); individuals in a variety of industries are taking thirteen-week sabbatical leaves; and a great many firms and industries encourage, if not require, early retirement. This is, of course, in addition to the fact that not so long ago we had a fifty, sixty, or even a seventy-hour work week, while today the average is below forty hours.

Couple these situations with the effects of technology and automation upon the homemaker, freeing her from the many previously time-consuming tasks in the kitchen and laundry alone, to say nothing of overall homemaking responsibilities. I frequently wonder how much the freeing of the homemaker's time has had to do with the rise of the feminist movement. Brightbill's prophetic character seemed to emerge again when he wrote in 1960 that "automation will spur and not impede the rate at which women are added to the labor force." His suggestion that labor-saving devices are as "clever at whipping up a batch of free time in the home" as they are in the highly automated factory is clearly seen in contemporary society.[4]

In addition to the time provided by labor-saving and time-saving devices in the home and on the job, we must also consider the reality of increased unemployment as it is currently emerging. Although this may be a sign of our economic times, I wonder if it is not related to an even greater phenomenon, the consequences of automation. According to Richard Kraus, author of several leisure-related texts, "some social scientists have actually estimated that within a few decades we might approach the point where two percent of the nation's workers would be able to produce all the goods needed for the entire population."[5] Could it be that many of our workers are simply not needed to produce what is required? If that is so, and these people are accurate in their assessment of the situation, what is to become of the rest of us?

Should you be tempted to scoff at the above forecast, let me remind you of only one of the current developments in industry—the robot. Identified by Westinghaus researchers as one of the seven scientific developments which will help solve the nation's productivity and energy supply problems, robots are emerging from the pages of science fiction and are beginning to transform the way the world works. One example of this is at Chrysler's Jefferson Plant in East Detroit where fifty robots have replaced two hundred welders who used to be on this assembly line. The robots work two shifts and have increased output by almost twenty percent; it is uncertain to what extent they have increased the unemployment statistic. It is surely *not* uncertain to what extent robots in the days ahead will do so.

What does seem certain is that the robot revolution promises to revive decaying industries and give smaller firms all the benefits of mass production without the human mass-producers. In addition, the American Society of Manufacturing Engineers and the University of Michigan forecast that:

    by 1985 20% of the labor in the final assembly of automobiles will be replaced by automation
    by 1987 15% of all assembly systems will use robot technology
    by 1988 50% of labor in small-component assembly will be replaced by automation
    by 1990 the development of sensory techniques will enable robots to approximate human capability in assembly.[6]

23 / *Hard Questions*

What does this forecast say to you? Surely you cannot continue to think that one day we will all be back to work!

Ultimately this robot revolution may also transform the way our society itself is organized and the way it assesses value. James S. Albus, head of robotics research at the National Bureau of Standards, was quoted in *Time* as saying, "The human race is now poised on the brink of a new industrial revolution that will at least equal, if not far exceed, the first Industrial Revolution in its *impact* on mankind."[7] What do you think he means by this?

Robots produce more for less, don't take coffee breaks, don't call in sick on Mondays, don't strike for higher wages and more benefits, don't make demands, don't get bored, or qualify for pensions. If, indeed, they can work faster, cheaper, with fewer mistakes, and for longer periods of time than their human counterparts, what will happen to the human workers? Robot makers answer, "They will be retrained." But by whom? And for what? The idea persists that human beings are destined for higher things, things intrinsically human, but what has been our preparation for this? And what are we speaking of when we call for things "intrinsically human"? Scientific research? Sports? Entertainment? Social work? Lying on the beach?

Are we prepared for the possibility of this *abundance* of free time? Perhaps Kraus's forecasting social scientists just may have been accurate in their prognosis.

If so, and this new age of leisure is actually upon us, it is not only a very sobering thought, but a disquieting one too—at least I find it so. It frightens me, even alarms me, when I think of how little most of us have prepared for the possibility of extensive free time. Do you recall from your history books what happened when this took place in ancient Rome? The Romans also had an abundance of free time, as over half the calendar year became holidays. Eventually they were presented with close to two hundred days of games and spectacles a year, and they became engaged in almost full-time spectatorship.

> Competitive sport . . . had become completely commercialized and professionalized. To maintain political popularity and placate the bored masses, the . . . senate provided great parades . . . bankrupting both the public treasury and private fortunes. . . . Audiences sometimes totaled half the adult populations of their cities. The . . . games were a visible dramatic illustration of lust for power, as well as preoccupation with brutality and force. . . . Shows were often lewd and obscene, leading to mass debauchery, corruption, and perversion of the human spirit. Over all, their vulgarity, cruelty, and lack of humanity reflected the spirit of the . . . people. . . . Historians have concluded that a major reason for the downfall of (the civilization) was that it was unable to deal with leisure; its citizens grew physically weak and spiritually corrupt. Although they were great engineers, soldiers, builders and administrators, they did not have the coherent philosophy of life that the ancients . . . had. When faced by the challenge of excess wealth, luxury and time, as a nation, they responded by yielding to corruption—and ultimately lost the simple virtues that had made them great as a nation.[8]

Do you wonder why I might be alarmed? Or are you tempted to say "this will never happen to us"?

You see, in leisure may well lie the final test of our society as we know it. To a great extent it was the abuse of the abundance of free time that led to the demise of the Roman Empire, and it is frightening to note the unquestionable similarity between Rome and the United States. As an exercise in comparison, study carefully the above paragraph, substituting "America" wherever "Rome" is meant. You will no doubt discover, as I did, that not a single passage will seem inappropriate. Like the Romans, Americans have become a nation of spectators, living life vicariously, whether in the form of watching televised "soaps" or commercialized competitive sports.

Nor is it simply the spectatoritis that is of concern to me; it is the awful complacency—the passive acceptance—with which we allow vulgarity, brutality, corruption and perversion to invade
> our homes,
>> our thinking,
>>> our very lives!

And we seem not even to notice.

If, indeed, the historians were correct in their conclusion that a major contributor to the downfall of Roman civilization was its inability to deal with leisure, why is it that we think this will not also be true for us?

Noted authorities in the field of leisure studies point out that, "Though our economic and industrial progress is dependent upon work, our cultural, moral and spiritual development is dependent, in large measure, upon uses of leisure." They further contend that "History has shown us that the world progresses or regresses not so much through what is done in our work hours but through what is done or not done in our leisure." From their perspective, and I agree, the "wise use of the gift of leisure is the challenge of our time."9

This means we must find new ways to give meaning and substance to our lives in our leisure. We must decide what kind of life we want. Will we be satisfied with the great American pastime of watching things happen? Do we desire merely the amusement and entertainment found in spectator sports, leisure parks, and our television sets? Surely to "know the meaning and purpose of life" (Ephesians 5:15–16) suggests otherwise, and as Christians, we must, for a change, lead the way! It is time for *us* to set the pace instead of follow it, to stem the tide rather than ride it.

> *Does* nothing phase us any more?
> *Have* we been lulled into passivity and permissiveness?
> *Are* we prepared for the possibility of an *abundance* of free time?
> Technology *has* improved our existence by making it easier, but
>
> *what of the quality of our lives?*

2 | "Define It – and Spell It"

Even as a young child, words held an incredible fascination for me, and I would occasionally demonstrate my latest vocabulary acquisition in a rather offhand manner during family dinner conversation. Apparently I did this fairly often, somewhat to the consternation of my family. I recall one such occasion when my brother, eight years my senior, challenged the use of my latest four-syllable word with, "Okay, Runt, (Can you imagine that for a nickname? No wonder I was held captive by words!) define it—and spell it!" Pausing a moment to gather my thoughts, I responded with something akin to "earth-shattering, of great consequence—sort of catastrophic I think—" and then proceeded with "c-a-t-a-c-l-y-s-m-i-c." We discussed it briefly, and since I had apparently used the word at least somewhat correctly, our conversation continued.

My big brother taught me a lesson that day—a lesson I have never forgotten. Definitions *are* important, if we're going to communicate effectively. Since it is my desire to do just that, it seems appropriate to define a few of the terms related to our discussion in this book. In that way we'll all have the same perspective.

Leisure is one of those words that conjures up all sorts of things in one's imagination: fooling around, lying in a hammock, being lazy, playing sports. Some people find it either a very amusing idea—or a shocking one! Others somehow associate it with people who "have more money than they know what to do with!" And then there are those whose imaginations simply cannot conceive of any such thing as leisure; it is a totally foreign concept.

Interestingly enough, the responses above rather closely, if loosely, dovetail with the four most commonly held views of leisure found in the majority of leisure-related textbooks: (1) the view of leisure as any non-work activity, any *activity* carried on during free time—a rather popular idea for many of us; (2) the "classical" view of leisure as exemplified in the writings of sociologist Sebastian deGrazia and the Swiss Catholic philosopher, Josef Pieper, where leisure is understood as a state of being involving a spiritual and mental attitude, the achievement of an inner calm or tranquility; (3) the view of leisure as a symbol of social class, an idea promoted by Thorstein Veblen, an American sociologist who wrote *The Theory of the Leisure Class* toward the end of the nineteenth century; and (4) the view of leisure as free, unobligated *time,* or that time left over after work and other binding responsibilities are cared for.

Time left over. What does *that* mean, you ask. If you are like many people I know, you find this a nearly impossible idea, and may well join the numerous individuals who say to me, "I don't need to know what to do with my leisure; I just need to find some! Tell me how to do that, and I'll be grateful." Well, maybe we'll attempt to do just that a bit later, but for now let's clarify what this commodity is that we desire so much.

Essentially our daily lives can be divided into three dimensions: existence time, subsistence time, and free time.

29 / "Define It—and Spell It"

Existence time would include sleeping, preparing and eating meals, bathing, grooming, and any other activities directly related to our biological existence. Subsistence time includes working, commuting to work, going to school and studying, or anything related to making a living or preparing to do so; homemaking tasks would also be included here. The time that remains is free time, or what some people term leisure.

Richard Kraus, to whom we have referred earlier, is one of those who regards leisure as unobligated or discretionary time. Apparently seeing some problems with this, he also introduces the idea of something designated as "semi-leisure." According to Kraus, Joffre Dumazedier suggests in *Toward a Society of Leisure* that "activities in which there is a degree of . . . obligation or purpose be regarded as 'semi-leisure.' Semi-leisure occurs when the world of work and of primary obligations partially overlaps with the world of leisure."[1] He goes on to explain that some uses of one's free time, such as reading in one's professional field or entertaining business contacts, may have work-related value, just as attending evening classes may improve one's work competence. If we couple these activities with the various nonwork occupations that have a degree of obligation about them (serving on the local school committee, being Sunday school superintendent), we discover exactly what he means. "In terms of time, energy, or degree of commitment, it would be difficult to distinguish such activities from work."[2]

I am sure that many of us would agree that commitment and obligation make at least part of our free time "semi-leisure," but what about the remainder? Surely there is some discretionary time left after we have gone about our daily subsistence and existence tasks, and have, additionally, contributed to the life of our church or community. (If such is not the case, I refer you to chapter 8, perhaps immediately!) What of this free, unobligated time? Is it leisure?

From my perspective, and for our consideration in discussion, this free time, in order to be considered leisure, must also take on other characteristics. Freedom to choose and freedom to be must also be a part of this discretionary time, for how can we call it discretionary if there is no freedom to decide, if there are no choices to make? Freedom is inherent in leisure, and certainly we must mean more than merely freedom from the coercion to work. Implied in the concept of leisure must be a freedom of personal choice and decision making.

Further, there should be little obligation and minimal compulsion for unobligated time to be considered leisure. It is an attitude toward this free time that makes it leisure, an attitude which lays claim to this period of time as our *own*, at our unique disposal, to be used at our discretion. There are no strings attached. This means we are not only free to make choices, but we *know* we are free to do so.

Basically, then, leisure may be defined as that period of time in an individual's daily life which is devoted neither to existence nor subsistence needs, and which may, therefore, be considered unobligated or discretionary time. It implies an attitude of freedom, especially freedom of choice.

Speaking of freedom, one area of our existence in which we experience rather significant freedom is our style of living, or what is commonly termed lifestyle. One would assume that we all know what is meant by this, but thinking back to the dinner table and my brother, I am reminded that we had better define this, too, lest we fail to communicate effectively.

31 / "Define It—and Spell It"

Lifestyle, most visible in our leisure, can initially be defined as the manner in which we conduct our lives, but that is far too simple a definition for our purposes. Although it is accurate, it leaves too much unsaid, too much unidentified, unexpressed, and thereby overlooked. It is our lifestyle, you see, that is the medium which best reflects our values and our value system. It is the *true* expression of that upon which we base our lives, of that which is important to us. We may quite easily verbalize what we declare is meaningful, but it is the manner in which we live that bespeaks our values accurately, for not only does our lifestyle reflect our values, it is, in fact, predicated by them. We *are* what—and how—we live; our lifestyle is the indicator of what we hold dear.

Lifestyle is also the way we manage our resources, financial as well as personal. Upon what do we spend our money? How do we go about making purchases? How do we decide whether or not to

> buy?
> remodel?
> go abroad?

And how is it that we manage our personal resources? Where—and how—do we use our

> talents?
> abilities?
> gifts?

Lifestyle is expressed in the expenditure of our time and energy; it is the distinctive manner in which we invest these priceless commodities. I have often pondered what a precious gift is the gift of time, and the older I grow the more valued is my energy! How we choose to use these bestowments is a clear indication of our values, expressed in our lifestyles.

Finally, lifestyle may be defined in the way in which we form relationships, and our reasons for doing so. Our associations, as well as how and why we foster and develop them, provide a clear picture of how we view the worth of other human beings.

Lifestyle, then, is the manner in which we conduct our lives, based upon our value system, and reflecting those values in the management of our resources, the expenditure of our time and energy, and the establishment of our relationships. It is the clear, distinctive expression of what we hold dear.

Value system—what we hold dear. How appropriate to introduce the last of the terms to be defined, Christianity, for embodied in that word is surely the basis for my value system, the essence of all I hold dear. Christianity is another word that conjures up all sorts of descriptions or interpretations, so it is especially important that we clearly describe what is meant in this discussion. However, in an attempt to define Christianity, I have come to the conclusion that for me there is no succinct definition of the term, as often as we might find one provided. You can be certain it is not here defined as the mere "religion based upon the teachings of Jesus" as any dictionary would indicate. For me it is not simply a religion at all, but rather it encompasses the body of Christ, those individuals who have a personal relationship with the living Savior, the company of those who have trusted Christ as Savior and who are endeavoring to make Him Lord of their lives.

Christianity has a two-fold dimension as I perceive it; a personal relationship with God through His Son, Jesus, which is then exemplified in a walk of faith. A personal relationship with God through His Son, Jesus, is exactly that: a relationship—and a personal one. Christianity is not knowing something *about* God; it is knowing God in an intimate, dynamic relationship (person to Person) by means of the indwelling Christ. By walk of faith is meant

> a reliance upon God as a faithful, righteous, holy God who will care for our every need;
>
> a reliance upon Christ for forgiveness and redemption, His having paid the penalty for our sins in His death and resurrection;
>
> a reliance upon the Holy Spirit who dwells within us, to guide, convict, and comfort us in our day-to-day living.

Perhaps my perception of what it means to be a Christian, what it means to follow Christ, what it means to be enveloped in Christianity is best expressed in this personal response to Psalm 71.

> *O great God of my salvation;*
> *my rock of refuge,*
> *my strength, my stability,*
> *My strong fortress,*
> *my hiding place, my shelter,*
> *My only hope,*
> *my heart's fulfillment, my soul's delight.*
>
> *I come to You with shouts of praise;*
> *for Your steadfast Love,*
> *for Your righteousness—alone—*
> *for Your life poured out*
> *for my redemption,*
> *for grace unmeasured,*
> *boundless, free, eternal.*
>
> *I lean upon Your loving breast*
> *and find Your strength*
> *adequate for all my needs,*
> *and find Your Love*
> *deeper, sweeter than ever imagined,*
> *and find Your peace*
> *beyond my ken—or wildest dreams!*

> *I put my trust in You alone*
>   *and find my trust*
>   *neither disappointed nor betrayed,*
> *but completed*
>   *in the God of all faithfulness,*
> *Who alone is*
>   *my Refuge, my Fortress, my Hope!*

Leisure, lifestyle, Christianity—spelled correctly, succinctly defined. My brother would be proud of me!

Leisure, lifestyle, Christianity—frequently used terms, just as frequently misused and misunderstood.

Leisure, lifestyle, Christianity—thought by many to be totally unrelated, here perceived as intimately intertwined. For it is in our leisure, expressed in our lifestyles that we either live out
> or deny
>   our faith.

3 | "No, Thank You"

> Let me burn out for Thee, dear Lord,
>   Burn and wear out for Thee;
> Don't let me rust, or my life be
>   A failure, my God, to Thee . . .
> Use me, and all I have, dear Lord,
>   And get me so close to Thee
> That I feel the throb
>   Of the great heart of God,
> Until I burn out for Thee.
>   Bessie F. Hatcher

Oh, how I loved that song, and with what sincerity and earnestness I would sing it! It was, in fact, a cherished theme of mine, and I would ponder the words carefully and often. I was serious about my walk with God, and there was nothing I desired so much as to live for Him, to be used by Him, and to have my life consumed in serving Him. There was simply no way that I wanted my life to be wasted, in any sense of the word. It was my passion to live and work for my Lord, and nothing else really mattered very much. To be sure, it seemed important to be a well-rounded individual, so there was a variety of expressions in my life, but all were entered into with great gusto and there were adequate commitments

to keep several people busy, not just one! Life was full and challenging and varied,
>> and hectic,
>> and rushed,
>> and breathless.

There were endless demands—as well as requests—and it all seemed so exciting and important and worthwhile. The dimensions of my life I described as three-fold: my personal commitments, my professional involvements, and my ministry. All were seen as overlapping and were equally important in living out my life for God. Life was full and challenging and varied,
>> and hectic,
>> and rushed,
>> and breathless.

In every dimension of my life I desired to honor God: it was important to be a good daughter, sister, friend, meaning extensive commitments of time and energy in each capacity, and leaving little time for myself. It seemed necessary to be the best teacher possible in my classes at the university, as well as a contributing member of the profession, meaning hour after hour spent in research and lecture preparation, endless committee meetings, and extensive conference contributions. It was imperative that I avail myself of every opportunity to share the Lord, meaning long hours in the office with students, and accepting whatever speaking engagements would fit into my schedule. Life was full and challenging and varied,
>> and hectic,
>> and rushed,
>> and breathless.
>>> And I was growing weary.

At least, I was weary every time I stopped long enough to know what I was feeling.

"No, Thank You"

So weary was I from overwork and overinvolvement, that at the prime of my life, and of my career as well, I very nearly did burn myself out—and for God—or so I thought. It was extremely difficult for me to comprehend my physician's words when I consulted him because of severe chest pains. "You are exhausted to the point of collapse," said he, "and must stop everything—all activity, your work, whatever involvements you have . . . (If he only knew!) Everything must be cancelled for at least six weeks, and then we'll reevaluate and decide what comes next. (Decide what comes next?) You are to leave town and go where no one can reach you. (That almost seems welcome.) You must have a complete rest—and I mean complete! Continue your daily swimming, but *nothing* else."

How could this have happened? I was doing only what I thought was right and good for anyone who loved God, who wanted to "burn out" for Him.

Thus, the evaluation began,
                       and the reexamination,
                       and the searching,
                       and the prioritizing,
                       and the changes.

Oh, but there had to be changes! Changes became imperative because careful examination of the Scriptures indicated that there are no instances in the Word which suggest that God's people should burn or wear themselves out, but rather that we should be good stewards of all we possess, and "all" includes our persons!

Thus, the concept of leisure in light of biblical Christianity entered my thinking. Some very basic questions had to be answered for me, as perhaps they must be for you.

How, we might ask, does the description of leisure presented in the preceding chapter conform to a biblical

perspective? How can we possibly think of having free, unobligated, discretionary time as Christians in a needy world, let alone such times in which we are free—free to choose, to do as we please, to be? How do we maintain our sense of responsibility?
of commitment?
of obedience?

Although I had been a professional in the field of leisure studies for many years, answering these questions became paramount for me; for although I understood leisure as an extremely important dimension in an individual's life, I seemed to have difficulty defending it for myself, a committed Christian, desiring to be used by God—unreservedly. It caused a tremendous tension within me as I grappled with the well-known Protestant work ethic and with what I understood to be the importance of leisure for one's mental health and general well-being. I can well appreciate the dilemma many of you may face as you consider the concept of leisure in your own lives.

Most of us understand leisure in relation to work. This is not at all difficult to comprehend when we observe the development of our once agrarian and now highly industrialized nation, for it was in such an evolution that the exaggerated value afforded work was established. Whether or not it is "human nature" which determined this I would not venture to say; there simply is evidence indicating that this inordinate emphasis on the worth of work does exist. It seems that the drives to work or to play are determined by one's culture, and the driving impulse to work appears to have been a governing factor for most of our society down through the years. The Christian emphasis has been lodged firmly in this drive to work, and we find it difficult to disengage ourselves from this perspective. One might say that we are stuck in the mire of work and productivity. My observation is that this sometimes takes on the quality of quicksand: the more one tries to free oneself, the more deeply entrenched one becomes.

As Harold Lehman, Mennonite leader and professor of education at Madison College in Harrisonburg, Virginia, points out in his book, *In Praise of Leisure,* we tend to separate work and leisure into disputant opposites, failing to see them as complementary elements in our lives, each making its unique contribution to our fulfillment as human beings. Instead, we measure the value of our leisure on the basis of work values, and we transfer to our leisure the drive for accomplishment and productivity. I know that I, for one, had done that. Could this be true in your life as well?

There seems to be little doubt that in contemporary society we are seeing a shift from the primary emphasis on work to the onset of an emphasis on leisure, yet we have established no values in regard to leisure; especially is this true of the Christian community. Few of us view leisure in a very positive light, and even fewer see it as the priceless gift it is—God's gift to us revealed in creation. Therefore, we squander it in the frenetic drive for usefulness and productivity.

God's gift to us revealed in creation—leisure?

> *In the beginning God created the heavens and the earth. . . . God saw all that he had made, and it was very good. And there was evening, and there was morning—the sixth day. . . . On the seventh day he rested from all his work. And God blessed*

> *the seventh day and made it holy, because on it he rested from all the work of creating that he had done.*
> Genesis 1:1, 31; 2:2–3

How is it that *leisure* is God's gift to us revealed in creation?

First we must recognize that we are made in God's image and, therefore, are to reflect His characteristics, His personage. We are admonished in the Word to emulate God: "Be imitators of God, therefore, as dearly loved children" (Ephesians 5:1). Volumes have been written concerning the attributes of God and how these apply to our individual lives, but little has been written, to my knowledge, which refers to the one dimension of God about which we are here concerned:

> God rested.
> God purposefully stopped working.
> God had leisure!

Can you imagine? *God had leisure!* And we are to imitate Him!

Contemplate with me, if you will, these verses from Genesis:

> *In the beginning God created the heavens and the earth. . . . God saw all that he had made, and it was very good. And there was evening, and there was morning—the sixth day.*

The Creator saw what He had made and deliberately stopped to enjoy it. *He deliberately stopped—to enjoy it.*

> *On the seventh day he rested from all his work.*

The Creator, Lord God of the Universe, very God of very God, rested. *He who never needed to—rested.*

> *And God blessed the seventh day and made it holy, because on it he rested from all the work of creating that He had done.*

The Creator, the One who made days and months and seasons revered a block of time *because He who had no need of it—had leisure on that day.*

41 / "No, Thank You"

God's gift to us revealed in creation—leisure. How is it we refuse to accept it? How do we say "No, thank-you" to God?

As a matter of fact, not only do few of us regard leisure as the precious gift from God that it is, but many of us rather consistently ignore God's admonitions to have leisure as they are sprinkled throughout the Word—or at least I managed to for many years. I'm not at all sure how I so conveniently overlooked the many passages that have to do with

    being still,

             and resting,

                        and being quiet.

Perhaps it was that I was so busy that I had little time for paying attention to my Father's exhortations. Perhaps I had become so lost in being used by God that it was nearly impossible to be found quiescently before Him. It appeared that I was too busy to listen quietly and well to anyone, even God. Yet His Word was clear and demanded my response.

Be still before the Lord and wait patiently for Him.
                                                    Psalm 37:7

Be still and know that I am God.
                                                   Psalm 46:10

This is what the Sovereign Lord, the Holy One of Israel, says:
  "In repentance and rest is your salvation,
  in quietness and trust is your strength,
  but you would have none of it."
                                                   Isaiah 30:15

Yes, the Word of God is clear and demands a response. Is it possible that you and I will have none of it? Can it actually be that we will look into the face of the Lord we love and say,

"No, thanks."
  No repentance,
    no rest,
      no quietness,
        no trust.
"No, thanks."
  No being still,
    no waiting patiently,
      no knowing You
        as You would have me know You.
"No, thanks;
  I choose to disobey."

Choose to disobey? God forbid. Yet to take no time to be still before the Lord; to have no leisure to know that He is God; to refuse to repent, to rest, to be quiet, and to trust Him is to disobey Jehovah God. Daily "quiet time" with little tranquility in one's life is not what He asks. Doing much for God with little quiescent being in Him is not what He desires. Knowing about God is not necessarily to know Him. "No short cut exists. God has not bowed to our nervous haste nor embraced the methods of our machine age," wrote A. W. Tozer. "It is well that we accept the hard truth now: *the man who would know God must give time to Him.*"[1] *Be still,"* He says, "and know that I am God" (emphasis mine). That indicates to me that quiet is a prerequisite to knowing God.

God has given us the gift of leisure, and He admonishes us to use it!

As if that weren't enough to convince me that the Lord wants us to have leisure, I found His provision for our pleasure in it clearly revealed in Paul's first letter to Timothy:

Hope in God, who richly provides us with everything for our enjoyment.   1 Timothy 6:17

God has provided us with the gift of leisure; He desires that we avail ourselves of it, and on top of that, He wants us to enjoy it! There is no guilt there, no wondering if we should take the time, no putting down the sheer enjoyment of life—including our leisure! The One who said, "I have come that they may have life, and have it to the full," (John 10:10) meant it. As Rudolph Norden put it in *The Christian Encounters the New Leisure:*

> Christian vocation . . . is the calling to the God-pleasing use of all of life's God-given gifts in all situations. The divine gifts enriching life include time in general, leisure as a special kind of time, and things that enter into the Christian's use of free time. The very idea of leisure as uncommitted time suggests . . . freedom, convenience, ease. Leisure is thus a gift God has given us to *enjoy*. . . . A golden text for the theology of leisure is 1 Timothy 6:17. In this passage Paul bids Timothy to urge the rich to cease trusting in 'uncertain riches' and to place their trust . . . in 'God, who generously gives us everything for our enjoyment.' (Phillips)
>
> The divine authorship, the abundance of all-inclusiveness of God's blessing are points to be especially noted. God is a Giver extraordinary. . . . He initiated a series of givings in a special way by first giving Himself. . . . He gave His only-begotten Son. . . . Now, the logic of revelation continues. . . . If God gave His own Son, shall He not also freely give us all things? The reply, as Paul emphasizes to Timothy, is decidedly in the affirmative: God 'giveth us richly all things to enjoy.'
>
> 'All things': this is all-inclusive. The gift of leisure is included. Consequently, in paraphrase the statement reads: 'God giveth us richly all leisure to enjoy.' It is not His purpose to vex or burden His people when He gives them leisure. The gift is intended for their delight and pleasure. . . . leisure is given them for enjoyment.[2]

Thus the questions asked earlier in this chapter are answered; leisure *does* conform to a biblical perspective.

Scripture indicates that it is a very special gift from an all-wise, all-loving, all-providing God.

We *can*, in fact, we *must*, have free, unobligated, discretionary time as Christians in a needy world, time in which we are free: free to choose, to do as we please, to be. We are *admonished* to have such time, for how else can we come to the needy world as healthy, whole, integrated individuals who know—really know—the triune God? It is in *availing* ourselves of this leisure that we maintain our sense
of responsibility,
of commitment,
of obedience.
By living "life with a due sense of responsibility, not as those who do not know the meaning and purpose of life but as those who do," (Ephesians 5:15–16 PHILLIPS) we are *committed* to *obedience,* even to obeying God when He says, "Be still . . . have leisure . . . and know that I am God."

Oh, by the way, my life remains full and challenging and varied, yet now it is also
quiet,
and deliberate,
and delightful.
And I am resting in my Beloved.

Those who cling to worthless idols,
forfeit the grace that could be theirs.
Jonah 2:8

4 | Salt Without Savor

"When are you coming to Japan? I just know you have it in the back of your mind somewhere!"

A friend penned those words on an airform to me during the six-month recuperation period following my aforementioned illness. My physician had urged me, upon resumption of my duties at the university, to spend some time away from my usual endeavors and responsibilities, and to do something I had always wanted to do. Since my friend was right, I had had a trip to Japan in the back of my mind, I followed up on her invitation, and before I knew it, I was embarking upon one of the most exciting experiences of my life—a sabbatical leave from the university, to be spent in Japan.

As I planned the trip, it was my threefold aim to become as immersed in the culture as possible in the few months I would be there; to study the leisure attitudes and values of the Japanese; and to spend the days in "quietness and trust" as I undertook my solo journey to the Far East. After some time alone in Hong Kong, I would spend the first six weeks in Japan with my friends; for the remainder of the time there I would be on my own. It was my prayer that God would stretch me in every dimension of my life, and that I would especially get to know Him better in our extended time alone together.

God most assuredly answered my prayer. I didn't know there were so many dimensions to my life which needed stretching! Every one of my senses was absolutely bombarded on this journey, to say nothing of the extent to which my emotions were stirred, my intellect stimulated, my body challenged, my social graces expanded, and my spiritual insights awakened. It was exciting to see the Lord answer my request and to so graphically illustrate to me just how varied, complex and full of wonder is the human experience as orchestrated by the One who designed it all. Surely He expanded my horizons beyond my comprehension.

As the time in Japan drew to a close, it seemed not only important, but imperative, that I engage in a period of reflection in order to retain, or at least try to retain, all I had experienced. Thus I spent eight days in a remote area of Maui, Hawaii—resting, relaxing, reflecting. As I endeavored to sort out experiences and impressions, I realized that, as a result of my encounters in Japan, I had gained new insight into the awesome truth expressed in the Psalms: how senseless and futile to worship man-made gods! We simply become as they are, blind, unfeeling, lifeless.

> *Their idols are silver and gold,*
>   *made by the hands of men.*
> *They have mouths, but cannot speak,*
>   *eyes, but they cannot see;*
> *they have ears, but cannot hear,*
>   *noses, but they cannot smell;*
> *they have hands, but cannot feel,*
>   *feet, but they cannot walk;*
>   *nor can they utter a sound with their throats.*
> *Those who make them will be like them,*
>   *and so will all who trust in them.*
>   Psalm 115:4—8

Indeed, how senseless and futile to worship man-made gods—any man-made gods! We simply become as they are:
blind,
    unfeeling,
        lifeless.
           In a word, dead.

How clearly was this seen in the Japanese culture. Silent and unresponsive, neither seeing nor hearing, beautifully formed bronze and gold images stared lifelessly into space as worshipers clapped their hands, offered them coins, and struck the temple gongs for their attention. I looked at those *dear* people and saw the damned—cleverly blinded by Satan. How striking is the evidence in our own society that Satan is blinding us rather effectively too, as we construct our own idols, faithfully serve them, and in the end become like them!

What, you may ask, do idols have to do with the topic of this book? Good question. The answer lies in the heart of the book itself; any discussion of lifestyle would be incomplete without addressing the topic of idols, for nowhere can they be seen more clearly than in the manner in which we live. We have only to recall our definition of lifestyle to understand this; it is the clear, distinctive expression of what we hold dear—of what we idolize, perhaps?

The definition of "idol" given by British sociologist and scholar J. A. Walter, in his book *Sacred Cows*, seems especially suitable to our discussion: "The word 'idol' means 'an object of love, admiration, or honour in an extreme degree' (Chambers Twentieth Century Dictionary), but it also implies a *false* object, not worthy of such admiration."[1] He then goes on to say, "The introduction of this highly evaluative term into the discussion is valid . . . within the

Judaic-Christian framework in which only God himself is worthy of worship and anything else commanding ultimate commitment is a false god or idol."[2] As he develops his thought, I am especially struck with his view that although idols are very personal, "they are also a thoroughly *sociological* phenomenon." People do not randomly or capriciously choose their idols; the idols they worship clearly reflect the society in which they live. Walter goes on to point out that "it takes a brave or original person to abstract himself from these and set up his own."[3]

This book is calling for the "brave and original" person to be just that, courageous and nonconforming; to dare to be different, to dare to go against the tide, to be his or her own person before God. Where are those who will deviate from the norm, who will boldly and deliberately turn away from the idols placed before them by society? Where are those who will determine in their hearts to worship only the triune God, who alone is worthy of our commitment and devotion? Although we are members of a society which has set up a variety of shrines and altars begging for our worship, it is time that we, as Christians, make decisions not at the dictate of society, but at the bidding of the indwelling Holy Spirit.

As a matter of fact, that is exactly what this chapter is all about: our response to society's dictate that we worship at the shrine of conformity and appearance.

Although we have been admonished in the Word, "Do not conform any longer to the pattern of this world" (Romans 12:1), or as Phillips paraphrases it, "Don't let the world around you squeeze you into its own mold," we have somehow paid little attention to this admonition—or at least so it seems. If we are to make a difference in our society we must *resolve* to *obey* our Lord in this exhortation, for hardly a day goes by without persistent pressure to conform to the standards and ideas of the world around us. Such pressure is imposed upon us (let us not be fooled into thinking otherwise) by the adversary via the media.

The adversary?

Satan?

Isn't that insinuating a great deal? Maybe. But if God says, "Do not conform" and another says, however subtly, "Conform," who is it? Who, more than he, would be interested in what is happening to the family structure in our nation?

In the reshaping of a value system away from the standards and principles for living set forth in the Word by our Creator?

In a code of religiosity and piety rather than dynamic transformation within to the image of Christ?

Make no mistake. Society and the media may be the vehicles by which we are carried to the idol of conformity and appearance, but it is an altar conceived by Satan. If those of us who name the name of Christ can be convinced otherwise, can be cajoled into thinking that much of what the world espouses today is "not all that bad," then not only will the adversary have succeeded in building his altar for our worship, but he will also have succeeded in getting us to worship there! To say nothing of the fact that he has used us, ourselves, to build it!

The idol of conformity and appearance is subtle indeed.

The most obvious place in which we conform to the dictates of society is in the family structure. Consider the types of family units presented on television, in the movies, or for that matter, in your child's second-grade reader. Gone are the traditional families, with father working to provide for the needs of his family, mother staying at home to make a *home,* and children being nurtured in an environment of security and love (not compensation, sentimentality, over-indulgence). Instead, we see single parents, family break-up via divorce (and often remarriage with a merging of two or more families), and increasing representation of "alternative lifestyles." Is it any wonder, then, that a mere 13 percent of the nation's families include the "traditional" family? That eighteen million children live in single-parent homes? That 64 percent of all children between three and five years old spend part of their day in child-care facilities? That more than 2.7 million single men and women cohabitate?[4] That homosexual activity is on the increase?

The subtle, persistent pressure to conform—to which we yield.

In addition, we see the roles of family members drastically changing as they are projected on the screen, to say nothing of male-female relationships. Gary Clarke, who writes about television for *Time* magazine, had this to say about the women we watch on television:

> Now, in the '80s, a new woman seems to have charged onto the tube. She's bold and brash, and . . . in the war between the sexes, she's practically Superwoman. No man gets the better of her . . . The new woman as heroine is not only more biting and sarcastic than other women in her show, she's stronger than any of the men around her. . . .
>
> This series, like so many I saw, implied—under its breath—that women can be equal only by downgrading men. . . . No matter what the situation, the secret of the

popularity of . . . these very popular shows is that the male archetypes are . . . merely ignorant . . . it's kind of sad that as the women on TV get smarter, the men get dumber and dumber.

. . . mostly missing from the TV screen is the married woman . . . None of them struck me as being even remotely as persuasive as the divorced and single woman I constantly saw on TV. Perhaps the message that the networks are trying to tell us is that not only is marriage no longer a joke, it is no longer even a sitcom.[5]

Even as the new woman has "charged onto the tube," so has she charged into the everyday of life. There is so little any more of the genteel, *truly* feminine woman who knows, because of the sheer wonder of being a woman, that she is equal, okay, even special. It is heartbreaking to me to see many of the young women with whom I work bulldozing their way into a situation, putting down the men in their lives, and arguing for their "rights." They vow not to marry, have children, and tie themselves down, ignoring the joy and fulfillment of family life and seeing only the loss of individual freedoms. And all the while, the young men not only do not seem to mind all that, but see themselves as contemporary, liberal, "liberated"—as they applaud the new woman, acquiesce to role reversal, and conform to society's dictates.

Nor is it just the younger generation. The idol of conformity and appearance has been erected by all of us, and we bow in submission as we see homes breaking up after years of happiness and commitment; parents failing to offer their children role models to respect and emulate; husbands and wives ignoring the design for marriage established by the One who made us male and female; many of us endorsing the so-called Equal Rights Amendment, the passage of which would *legalize* "*no* distinction between male and female and their respective roles."[6]

At the time of the final defeat of this amendment, ERA

supporters were quick to remind us that they were far from being permanently defeated. At this writing, great sums of money are being amassed for future legal battles over this issue. We can be sure that the ERA is far from being laid to rest. "ERA advocates are not simply supporting an amendment, they are promoting a movement," a movement for the "development of new sets of relationships between individuals and groups."[7]

The family structure is not the sole concern; of considerable consequence is what lies behind the changes in our family structure, the rampant permissiveness in our society. The deceptive allure of the idol of conformity and appearance also contributes to the reshaping of our entire value system. There is an insidious insistence hammering away at us that works to convince us that there simply are no absolutes, that everything in life is relative. As Christian writer Francis Schaeffer observes, "The nature of the universe depicted by modern science makes *unacceptable any supernatural* or *cosmic guarantees of human values*"[8] (emphasis mine). And we seem to resist not at all! We crumble under the hammering, for we have built our houses upon sand and not upon the Rock;

> we speak eloquently in words of compromise and confusion, and resist the example in Christ Jesus to speak with authority;
>
> we fear offending our friends and being rejected by them more than we desire to please the Lord.

No longer, therefore, do we establish our lives upon the absolutes set forth within the Word of God; we are even rather unacquainted with them—or so it seems. As a matter of fact, many of us, even as Christians, would find it difficult to define what we mean by "absolutes," and would find it equally troublesome to give an example. Thus, with the apparent endorsement of the Christian community, we have entered into what I term the era of a value system of no values. Some would title it, and rightly so, the Age of Humanism.

All about us we see the results of the infiltration of such a philosophy into our society; not one dimension of it is immune. It is expressed in government, our legal system, the breakdown of the family, in our leisure pursuits, our schools, our medical centers (perhaps especially our medical centers). Humanism has not only *invaded* our society, it has *conquered*
> the way we think,
>> view the world,
>>> make choices.

Christians, bowing to the idol of conformity and appearance, are doing little to stop this invasion. We seem fearful, impotent, and even worse, apathetic as we conform to society's dictates and follow a lifestyle that appears essentially no different from that of our non-Christian counterparts. Where is our resolve to *obey* the Lord?
> What difference are we making in maintaining the Judeo-Christian way of thinking upon which our country was founded?
>> With what values are we nurturing our children, illustrating to them the soundness of biblical truth?
>> Whatever happened to the salt of the earth? The light of the world?

Indeed, the subtle pressure to conform—to which we yield.

Speaking of salt and light, how is it that the salt seems to have lost its savor? That the light seems to be so well hidden in this age of darkness? Could it be that we have conformed to a code of religiosity and piety, thus *appearing* to be salt but having none of its qualities? Could it be that by involving ourselves in all sorts of religious activities and devout (but not necessarily godly) endeavors we have lost our brilliance? It is so easy (made so, I am sure, by the adversary) to become lost in conforming to a religious maxim rather than developing a godly life! Before we know it we have been taken "captive through hollow and deceptive philosophy, which depends on human tradition . . . rather than on Christ" (Colossians 2:8). Thus we become like the church in Ephesus, about whom it was said,

> *You have persevered and have endured hardships for my name, and have not grown weary. Yet I hold this against you: You have forsaken your first love.*
> Revelation 2:3–4

How easy it is to conform to a code of activity; how difficult to love by obeying! Yet John tells us in his first epistle, "This is love for God: to obey his commands" (1 John 5:3). Jesus Himself said, "If you love me you will obey what I command. . . . Whoever has my commands and obeys them, he is the one who loves me. . . . He who does not love me will not obey my teaching" (John 14:15, 21, 24). As Tozer so aptly put it in *That Incredible Christian;*

> So the final test of love is obedience. Not sweet emotions, not willingness to sacrifice, not zeal, but obedience to the commandments of Christ. Our Lord drew a line plain and tight for everyone to see. On one side He placed those who keep His commandments and said, "These love Me." On the other side He put those who keep not His sayings, and said, "These love me not."[9]

To love God, then, is to obey Him. It is to obey Him when He says, "Do not conform any longer to the pattern of this world"—no matter how beguiling or attractive the pattern! It is to obey Him when He says, "be transformed by the renewing of your minds"(Romans 12:2)—no matter how intellectually beguiling or spiritually attractive is the activity in which we are engaged!

Although it is imperative that we continually be *willing* for God to transform us, which takes work on our part, the transformation itself is God's work. It is done for us, not by us. We give God permission to transform us and then the work is His. All the activity in the world—even good, religious, devout activity—will neither transform our lives nor renew our minds. That is God's task, God's responsibility. Ours is to love Him by our obedience, and to worship Him alone.

God makes very clear in His Word what He thinks of activity and outward appearance. Jesus had this to say about the religious leaders of the day:

> *Everything they do is done for show. They act holy . . . woe upon you . . . you other religious leaders—hypocrites! For you tithe down to the last . . . but ignore the important things—justice and mercy and faith. . . . You are like beautiful mausoleums—full of dead men's bones, and of foulness and corruption. You try to look like saintly men, but underneath those pious robes of yours are hearts besmirched with every sort of hypocrisy and sin.*
> Matthew 23:5, 23, 27–28 LB

These words were spoken by our Lord to the religious people of that day. Were Jesus to walk among us now, I wonder what He would say to some of us about our contemporary code of religiosity, our busyness for God. Could it be that in our "working for the Lord" we are, in reality, bowing to the idol of appearance instead of obeying Him in our
    attitudes,
           relationships,
                 conversations,
                       values,
                            purpose?

Oh! the subtle pressure to conform—to appear—to which we yield.

The idol of conformity and appearance: one idol, two dimensions. I have purposefully chosen not to separate them because they seem to be so intertwined. Frequently, perhaps even usually, we conform in order to appear—or not to appear. We tend to follow along with the crowd, and it matters little which crowd, so that we blend in and do not stand out too much. We adopt societal values with little apparent concern for the consequences in order to appear knowledgeable, up-to-date, flexible. We fall in with what society dictates lest we appear too different, too "old fashioned," too unbending. We do our good deeds and busy ourselves with "Christian activity" to appear righteous, devout, even pious. We conform . . . in order to appear. Thus do we bow at—worship—the idol of conformity and appearance.

> *Their idols are . . .*
> *made by the hands of men. . . .*
> *Those who make them will be like them,*
> *and so will those who trust in them.*
> Psalm 115:4, 8

Like Them?
    Really like them?
        Lifeless?
           Dead?
That's what the Word says: like them.

5 | All Costs, Any Cost

When I was a senior about to depart from the hallowed halls of secondary school, one of the biggest deals was to be identified as one of the outstanding seniors pictured in the school yearbook. We all know the categories—most intelligent, most versatile, most athletic, most popular, most likely to succeed. I often wondered by what criteria we decided who was the most intelligent or most likely to succeed. Perhaps the former had something to do with the grades one received and the latter with just how industrious one appeared. At any rate, we voted, and it is somewhat doubtful whether or not we'll ever know how accurate we were!

Just for fun, I telephoned a recent high-school graduate to see if they still do this sort of thing. Sure enough, that is one tradition that seems to have been maintained these many years! I was especially interested in the category of "most likely to succeed" (maybe because I wasn't chosen for it!) and asked what criteria were given by which the students could make their decisions. It occurred to me, with the sort of sophistication currently displayed among high-school seniors, that things might have become more well-defined. I was wrong. "No criteria," said my informant. "We just vote."

"What criteria for 'most likely to succeed' did *you* use?" I asked.

"You know—talent—someone who's got it up there—ambition," was the reply.

Most likely to succeed: someone with talent, brains, ambition. Isn't that how most of us think of the person most likely to succeed? Someone "with it" who will "make it."

Why, among all the other adolescent-chosen categories of popularity, versatility, good looks, intelligence, and athletic ability, is the rather adult classification of success found? Could it be that we are in such a success-oriented society that the pressure to succeed hounds us from early childhood? Few of us are exempt. We are given the impression—sometimes quite subtly and sometimes quite directly—very early in our lives that it is not *who* we are that is important, but it is *what* we are that counts. We learn that our worth is clearly related to what we can do (and how well we can do it) and not to who we are as individuals, unique and precious and full of wonder, created in God's image. Overlooked completely is our real worth, indicated by Christ's redemptive love even when we sin. Instead we are taught to
        achieve,
      aim high,
          perform,
             be *successful*.
                Sometimes at any cost.
                Any cost.
Even at the price of our integrity,
    our family relationships,
                          our relationship with God.

With a great deal of care, deliberation and precision, the idol of success and achievement (synonymous words in

America) has been constructed. Few there are who have not worshiped at its altar. Men nearly abandon their wives and families for it, becoming compulsive achievers and workaholics; women place unreal demands upon themselves for it, frequently driving themselves to despair; children lie and cheat for it and learn early on that whatever it takes to be on top is okay as long as you don't get caught. It is more important to be a success in whatever the endeavor than to risk failure, whatever the resultant learning. "Success at all costs" has become our call to worship.

Our call to worship?
Indeed. Our call to worship at the shrine of success and achievement.

Strong statement? Perhaps. But have you stopped to consider with what we have equated success in contemporary society? Most of us think generally in terms of
accomplishment, achievement, attainment;
acquisition, accumulation, affluence.
To be successful, by today's standards, is to have *done* and to have *obtained*.

The idol of success and achievement is high and lifted up and greatly revered in the technological society in which we find ourselves. Loud are the anthems of worship: new ideas, bigger plans, greater productivity, marked efficiency, better promotion, increased sales! And the rewards for such adulation? Advancement and promotion, longer hours, more responsibility, higher salaries, less time with one's loved ones (but the ability to buy more for them), greater prestige. What an idol!

Not only do we sing its praises and bask in our ensuing rewards, but our allegiance to our country and even our devotion to God seem almost to be measured by our worship of this idol. Our patriotism is measured by our productivity; our good citizenship by our support of the economy. Nor is public spirit alone the demonstration of our devotion. Many Christians seem to feel that God's choicest blessings are in the form of wealth and accomplishment, and, in effect, espouse the idea that the best Christians are the most affluent: that one who is spiritual is also successful. As Christian psychiatrist Frank Minirth observes, "Many Christians today are living in $150,000 houses. They drive Cadillacs and their wives wear minks. These Christians have become successful, defining success as affluence. In their view, wealth is a sign of God's blessing."[1] *Surely* achievement and accumulation must be indicators of our interest in the welfare of our nation and the degree to which God has honored our devotion to Him, or why would we act as if they were?

Our success as a contributing member of society at large—and also as a Christian—becomes measured, then, by what we do and what we possess, not by the kind of individuals we are. It is measured

by our gains—financial and otherwise;
> by our goals—clearly and cleverly established and attained;
>> by our grit—exemplified by our exertion and determination.

Oh, yes, what an idol! And great is the praise of it!

Yes, great is the praise of it—as we plunge headlong into a pattern of striving, performance, productivity, and achievement that leads us directly into the well-respected (of tremendous significance in itself!) addiction of many individuals in contemporary society: workaholism. A term not even heard of twelve years ago, workaholism is now the subject of numerous articles and books. It is of especial interest to me that much of the material dealing with workaholism is written from a religious perspective. Wayne Oates, a professor of psychology of religion and a former pastor, coined the term "workaholic" and observed that work "can become the special addiction of the religious man. . . . we feel more religious the more we are addicted to work! The religious group tends to extol this form of addiction."[2]

The workaholic, an "individual who has a dependence on overwork, a dependence which has a noticeable disturbance on the rest of his life,"[3] may be applauded by many, even seen to be virtuous by some. The one so addicted to work will be no more applauded, honored, and venerated by his family for his work addiction, however, than will the drug addict for addiction to drugs or the alcoholic for alcohol dependence. The family knows the consequences. "The community in general sees the work addict only from afar, in terms of what he or she gets done, expressing 'oohs' and 'ahs' of amazement at the workaholic's accomplishment."[4] Never seen from afar are the crippling effects of this esteemed addiction, but surely those close to the one so addicted are accutely aware of the results. Communication with loved ones is greatly impaired, if not destroyed; conflict and turmoil arise within the home. The workaholic is
    so preoccupied,
            so wearied,
                      so overscheduled
that little else is of significance or even noticed. Spouses are neglected, children alienated, friends forgotten or overlooked.

And one's relationship with God? Perhaps this is the most neglected of all, even (maybe especially) among those involved in a ministry, for God is not present in the flesh to make demands (nor would He), to make visible overtures, to say, "Look at me, please look at me," the way our children do.

To the one addicted to work there are also consequences that the family may never be aware of except indirectly; notably is the consequence of never getting to really know oneself. If one can keep busy enough, perform up to standards and expectations, produce and achieve, one will never have to do much soul-searching. Many workaholics find this very comfortable. Psychiatrist Paul Meier points out in *The Workaholic and His Family* that many individuals become workaholics in the first place as they circumvent getting better acquainted with themselves.

> I am thoroughly convinced that one major reason why most workaholics *are* workaholics is to avoid insight into their innermost motives, emotions, insecurities and fears. I know of some workaholic friends who spend their entire vacation feeling miserable when they ought to relax and have fun. So they find some other work to do during their vacation. I know of one physician who took his family to the ocean for a vacation, but spent the whole time picking up tin cans and beer bottles off the cluttered beach. Had he relaxed, he would have started to get in touch with his repressed anger and gained painful insights into himself; so, to avoid gaining insights, he stayed busy like a good workaholic.[5]

Do you know anyone like that? Does it sound even remotely familiar?

Indirectly, of course, the family feels the consequences in this situation, too. The one addicted to work to avoid insights cheats the family by never allowing them to know the real person. The workaholic, male or female, is as isolated from loved ones as the alcoholic or drug addict. Make no mistake about that.

Success and achievement—what an idol! And great is the praise of it!

65 / All Costs, Any Cost

So great is the praise of it, in fact, that we often sacrifice our loved ones to it, especially our children. We venerate success, we loudly sing its praises, we let our children know, by our expectations and demands, that it is success we worship. And it is success that we want them to worship too, for after all, what good parent would not want to pass along the family gods? Even at the expense of the child.

> When the birth of their firstborn child draws near, they hope and pray that the baby will be normal—that is, "average." But from that moment on, *average will not be good enough*. Their child must *excel*. He must *succeed*. He must *triumph*. He must be the *first* of his age to walk or talk or ride a tricycle. He must earn a stunning report card and amaze his teachers. . . . He must star in Little League, and later on he must be the quarterback or the senior class president or the valedictorian. His sister must be the cheerleader or the soloist or the homecoming queen. *Throughout the formative years of childhood,* his parents give him the *same message day after day:* "We're counting on you to do something fantastic, Son, now *don't disappoint us!"*
>
> . . . the younger generation is our most reliable status symbol. Middleclass parents vigorously compete with each other in raising the best-dressed, best-fed, best-educated, best-mannered, best-medicated, best-cultured, and best-adjusted child on the block. The *hopes, dreams and ambitions of an entire family sometimes rest on the shoulders of an immature child.*
>
> . . . the vast majority of our children are not dazzlingly brilliant, extremely witty, highly coordinated, tremendously talented, or universally popular! They are just plain kids with *oversized needs to be loved and accepted as they are.* Thus, the stage is set for unrealistic pressure on the younger generation and considerable disappointment for their parents.[6] (Emphasis mine.)

So writes James Dobson, psychologist and noted authority on issues relevant to family life.

And thus do we sacrifice our children on the altar of success.

Nor is it our children only that we sacrifice. So great is the praise of success and achievement that the price of worship must also be paid with our very own persons as well. The glitter and brilliance of such an idol as this causes our vision to become distorted and we see things askew, out of focus. We have only to note our perception of the route to this shrine, the pathway to success. Often this pathway is filled with compromise and conformity, and the distortion caused by our devotion to success blinds us so we lose sight of our priorities. We sacrifice our personal lives for our success: we begin to do things we don't really believe in; we refrain from engaging in those endeavors which we have always held most dear.

Not long ago, I found myself in just such a myopic condition. When I arrived at the university, classroom instruction was of primary concern, and I had been assured by the dean in our initial interview that my effectiveness as a teacher would be the main criteria for evaluation. This was as I had hoped, for I was committed to teaching undergraduates, and to doing a good job of it. I had no interest in a position at an institution which would not honor quality teaching. This was my calling, this was my expertise; and I accepted my appointment based upon this understanding.

It was not long, however, before things began to change at our university, just as they were doing at others. The "sputnik era," as our dean calls it, came about and the great push was on for scientific research. That was hardly my cup of tea! As the time for my promotion and tenure decision year drew near, my department head drew me aside and spoke at great length of the necessity for me to engage in research, to publish more. We were now experiencing the "publish or perish" syndrome. Without more publications to my credit, as well as extensive research, there would be no promotion and surely no tenure.

What was I to do? Obviously, I was to set aside that to which I was committed, quality teaching, and devote myself to research and publication. After all, hadn't I a responsibility to follow the dictates of my superiors? Wasn't it important to be successful in whatever endeavor I undertook? Wasn't that being a good "witness?"

Each January our university has a "winterterm" during which time those of us on the faculty who are not teaching short courses are free to engage in academic endeavors for which we do not otherwise have sufficient time. Usually I spend this time reworking my courses, preparing new lectures, writing, doing library research and reading extensively to enhance my classroom involvement. The January following the aforementioned "tête-à-tête" with my department head, however, I planned to spend doing some research as a basis for publication. After all, hadn't I a responsibility to follow the dictates of my superiors?

I left town to engage in this scholarly pursuit, for I knew I would have to be where no one could reach or bother me. Little did I know that this was exactly what I needed for God to reach me, "bother" me, clear up my vision, and bring me to my senses!

That is exactly what took place. I was reminded that it was teaching, not research and publication, to which I was called; that it is the *people* God chooses to bring into my life in the classroom to whom I have a responsibility; that it is more important to be faithful to that to which God calls me than to be successful by the world's standards; and that being true to my convictions is a far greater "witness" than succumbing to the idol of achievement.

By reminding me of all that, God prompted me to spend my time in preparation for the new semester, for my classes and student involvement, and assured me that He would care for the rest. After all, didn't He promise to do just that sort of thing when He said,

> *So don't worry at all about having enough food and clothing. Why be like the heathen? For they take pride in all these things and are deeply concerned about them. But your heavenly Father already knows perfectly well that you need them, and he will give them to you if you give him first place in your life and live as he wants you to.*
>
> *So don't be anxious about tomorrow. God will take care of your tomorrow too.*
>
> Matthew 6:31–34 LB

Upon returning from that winterterm, I told my department head of my decision to continue with my first priority: quality teaching. He was disappointed that I had given up my plans for research and publication, for he saw it as "the kiss of death," but supported me in my decision. I assured him that I was at the university by God's appointment; if He wanted me there any longer I would receive my tenure, and if He didn't want me there, I didn't care to remain.

Little did I know that my Father was, indeed, caring for the rest. Unknown to me, I had been nominated for the Distinguished Teaching Award at the university. And just prior to my promotion and tenure decision, I was the recipient of that award. What administration would deny tenure to someone thus honored?

Obviously, God wanted me to remain. How thrilled I still am that He restored my vision!

What an idol! What a blinding, confusing idol! And great is the praise of it!

So great is the praise of it that it enters every area of our lives, and we bow in subservience as we carry it over into the realm of the spiritual. Not only do we strive to

>achieve,
>>aim high,
>>>perform,
>>>>be *successful* in our everyday endeavors,

we carry this same striving into our relationship with God. Our walk with Him becomes a burden and not a delight as we strive to achieve the status of "good Christian." We strive to perform well,
>achieve a "certain spirituality,"
>>"walk on the highest plane."

We strive to be *successful* Christians, whatever that means.

Instead of performance, is it not our heart's intent He desires? Did Jesus ever speak of a life at the pinnacle of bliss,
>with no temptations,
>>no problems,
>>>no pain?

Are not the true marks of the Christian the fruit of the Spirit described in Galatians 5? Love, joy, peace, patience, kindness, goodness, faithfulness, gentleness, and self-control; these are the marks of the Christian.

And these are *fruit*,
>a product,
>>the *result* of a walk with God.

As Tozer said in *That Incredible Christian,* "All this must be done by the operation of the Holy Spirit within . . . No man can become spiritual by himself. Only the free Spirit can make a man spiritual."[7] The Spirit is free, but we must avail ourselves of Him. As we give first priority to God, we become successful indeed; successful in the greatest sense of the word—and in accordance with the Word. We become successful in our manifestation of His fruit.

What a contrast between the success just described and the idol under our consideration!

And what a difference in cost! The cost involved in the former was cared for by our Redeemer. The price of worship at the shrine of success and achievement is personal and dear. If "success at all costs" has become our call to worship, this litany we chant seems to say it all:

> All costs, any cost, success is all that matters!
> New car, second home, executive position.
> All costs, any cost, success is all that matters!
> Frequent travel, latest clothes, pretty children—two.
> All costs, any cost, success is all that matters!
> Lots of laughter, not much joy, little time alone.
>
> All costs, any cost, success is all that matters!
> Deserted spouse, unhappy home, little gentle love.
> All costs, any cost, success is all that matters!
> Neglected children, not enough time, I don't even know them.
> All costs, any cost, success is all that matters!
> If God is there, I don't know where, I haven't time to find Him.
> All costs, any cost, success is all that matters. . . .

6 | Notebooks, Card Files, and Manila Folders

As I look back over the years spent in educational pursuits, there are many special experiences which stand out in my memory. Some are easily recalled because they were exceptionally challenging; some because they were especially stimulating; some because they were so absolutely ridiculous; and some simply stand out on their own, for no real reason except for their uniqueness. Such is an experience I had in graduate school as I was studying for my doctoral degree.

I was nearing completion of my academic courses and was about to launch into the nemesis of all graduate students, the dissertation. As if it weren't bad enough that I had to do all that research in the first place, it was necessary that I select a committee of senior faculty members whose task it would be to examine me upon the selection and proposal of a dissertation topic and then to reexamine me upon the final presentation of the research paper. This latter examination is called a "defense," and rightly so. Consequently, one goes about the selection of a committee with a great deal of care and deliberation.

The members of this austere group, in addition to faculty from my own department, were to be chosen according to their expertise in the area under consideration in the research. Since I was going to be involved in some rather sophisticated statistical analysis, it was suggested by my advisor that I select someone from the sociology department who was especially known for his statistical expertise. That way he could *really* examine my knowledge in this area! With some sense of awe and a great measure of trepidation, I called upon the individual whose name had been given me as the one most likely to fill the requirements for membership on my committee. We established a time when we could meet to discuss my upcoming perquisition and we began our brief association.

Since I did not know this individual, and since he was about to assume a great deal of responsibility pertaining to the attainment of my academic goals, I thought it wise to investigate, albeit casually and somewhat surreptitiously, something of his background and interests. We engaged in conversation pertaining to his academic experience and pursuits, focusing especially upon his specific areas of interest in the field of sociology. He told me of the various studies in which he had taken part—in which scholarly journals he had published. He elaborated a good deal on the current research in which he was involved. Obviously he was a scholar. It all sounded tremendously impressive to me, and I was eager to hear more about the studies and what was done with them. I now know it was naive of me to ask, but being less "knowing" then, I queried, "What, exactly, do sociologists *do* with all the findings from their studies?"

Somehow I knew I had asked either an inappropriate question or a terribly difficult one, for the answer was not quickly forthcoming. My about-to-be-on-my-dissertation-committee-very-recent-acquaintance was taking a great deal of time to form his answer to what I thought was an extremely simple question.

After what seemed to me to be several minutes, but in

reality I suppose was no longer than a few seconds, he replied, "That's a good question. Well, I guess you could say that mostly we just tell other sociologists about them. We publish the findings in journals, we give papers. Yes, I guess you'd say we just tell other sociologists."

As amusing as that may appear, isn't that precisely what many of us do every day? We pursue knowledge for knowledge's sake; we talk about things we *know*; we throw out quotations—sometimes biblical quotations—primarily to impress others.

We acquire
>facts,
>>data,
>>>trivia,
>>>>learning,
>>>>>with little application to our lives.
We acquire tremendous knowledge with little effect upon the inner man in each of us.

As a matter of fact, in our information-laden society, we worship at the ancient, well-beloved shrine of knowledge and information.

Ancient? Isn't this desire for knowledge a modern phenomenon? Hardly. Note, if you would, the following passage from Genesis.

> *Now the Lord God had planted a garden in the east, in Eden; and there he put the man he had formed. And the Lord God made all kinds of trees grow out of the ground—trees that were pleasing to the eye and good for food. In the middle of the garden were the tree of life and the tree of the knowledge of good and evil. . . .*
>
> *The Lord God took the man and put him in the Garden of Eden to work it and take care of it. And the Lord God*

> commanded the man, "You are free to eat from any tree in the garden; but you must not eat from the tree of the knowledge of good and evil, for when you eat of it you will surely die. . . .
>
> Now the serpent was more crafty than any of the wild animals the Lord God had made. He said to the woman, "Did God really say, 'You must not eat from any tree in the garden?'"
>
> The woman said to the serpent, "We may eat fruit from the trees in the garden, but God did say, 'You must not eat fruit from the tree that is in the middle of the garden, and you must not touch it, or you will die.'"
>
> "You will not surely die," the serpent said to the woman. "For God knows that when you eat of it your eyes will be opened, and you will be like God, knowing good and evil."
>
> When the woman saw that the fruit of the tree was good for food and pleasing to the eye, and also desirable for gaining wisdom, *she took some and ate it. She also gave some to her husband, who was with her, and he ate it. Then the eyes of both of them were opened* . . .
>
> Genesis 2:8—9, 15—17; 3:1—7 (emphasis mine)

When Eve saw that the fruit of the tree was not only good to eat and attractive to behold, but that it was also the sort of comestible whose consumption would lead to the attainment of a special sort of knowledge, the temptation simply became too great. She yielded to it on the spot, taking her husband into sin with her. The inordinate desire for knowledge was that which prompted the first members of all mankind to disobey God. Nor are we dissimilar to our hoary ancestors as we continue to consume ourselves with desire for knowledge and information; there is a telling family likeness.

So similar are we to our progenitors that although they first established this now ancient and venerated idol, we have sharpened our construction procedures and have become far more sophisticated and proficient in our modes of worship. We have discovered new and marvelous means of keeping abreast of "all there is to know" about a subject, having merely to press the appropriate buttons on the latest automated information device (sometimes known as a data bank) to obtain the most recent round of information on a given subject. To be unfamiliar with the procedure is unthinkable. To have one's offspring enrolled in an academic institution without such technological advantages is to have denied the child's right (previously known as a privilege) to learn in the most advanced and up-to-date manner. After all, one's knowledge and acquaintance with current information, regardless of the type or pertinence of it, is a sure indicator of one's intelligence and ability, to say nothing of its value as a predictor of one's success in life.

Or so it would seem.

Then, again, it would depend upon what is meant by intelligence, ability, success.

At any rate, knowledge and information, vastly different from much else in our lives, is something which we are all admonished, "cannot be taken away from you," so it is clearly legitimized and surely to be worshiped and revered above all else. That to which we can cling with such assurance *must* be important!

> But knowledge really is a good thing, isn't it?
> > Well, is it?
> > > In and of itself?

> Think about it: precisely what good is
> > knowledge without purpose?
> > > information without integration?
> > > > cognition without affect?
> > > > > acquisition without application?
> > > > > > ideation without action?
> > > > > > > trivia without meaning?

I propose that it is of little value. Perhaps of no value at all. God says, "I will destroy the wisdom of the wise; the intelligence of the intelligent I will frustrate" (1 Corinthians 1:19). Knowledge for its own sake serves little purpose except to give us something to cling to, something to venerate and worship, something to becloud the issues regarding what—or who—is truly worthy of our worship. There are many individuals who find it impossible to trust in Christ, for the message of the cross is so simple, so foolish-sounding, so narrow. "The preaching of the cross is, I know, nonsense to those who are involved in this dying world, but to us who are being saved from that death it is nothing less than the power of God" (1 Corinthians 1:18 PHILLIPS). It seems to some that it is so much more intelligent to follow the broader path of *knowledge.* Our information-laden, knowledgeable society bids us worship at the ancient, well-beloved shrine of knowledge and information.

Some of us who call ourselves Christians, who purport to have believed in the preaching of the cross, also follow the broader path of knowledge. To do so seems so much more convenient than to allow spiritual truth to be applied to and integrated into our daily lives (or why the unbelievers' continuing cry of "hypocrisy?"). It might even be said of the Christian community that this idol of knowledge is especially venerated by our little society as we go about gathering more and more information about God and greater and greater knowledge of His Word while all the while failing to appropriate the knowledge we already have. It is somehow of little import that we apply to our day-to-day living and integrate into our beings the information and knowledge of God that we have acquired via our

77 / *Notebooks, Card Files, and Manila Folders*

workshops,
    seminars,
        Bible studies,
            Sunday morning sermons.
It appears much more meaningful to have this knowledge tidily held in
        notebooks,
           card files,
                manila folders,
than to have it muddy our lives by attempted application!
    It is far easier, as we bow to knowledge and information, to diagram, discuss, and doctrinize,
        than to delight in, dwell upon, and *diligently obey*
            the precious Word of God.

    What has happened to the *authority* of God's Word? To *obedience* to the Word in our daily lives? Could it be that we have become so misdirected in the maze of intellectual pursuit of the Scriptures that we fail to notice how completely we have lost our bearings? How is it that we can approach the Word of God as we would any other fascinating piece of ancient literature, dissecting the passage under consideration, parsing the very Word of Jehovah God, reducing the Scriptures to an analytical, intellectual exercise? Of what real purpose is the tearing apart of Holy Writ, piece by piece, other than to inform, to fill up notebooks, to buttress the hollow faith of those within hearing!
    A. W. Tozer presents a similar thought in his penetrating book, *That Incredible Christian:*

> For a long time I have believed that truth, to be understood, must be lived; that Bible doctrine is wholly ineffective until it has been digested and assimilated by the total life. . . . A theological fact may be held in the mind for a lifetime without its having any positive effect

> upon the moral character; but truth is creative, saving, transforming, and it always changes the one who receives it into a humbler and holier man.
>
> At what point, then, does a theological fact become for the one who holds it a life-giving truth? *At the point where obedience begins.* . . .
>
> Theological facts are like the altar of Elijah on Carmel before the fire came, correct, properly laid out, but altogether cold. When the heart makes the ultimate surrender, the fire falls and true facts are transmuted into spiritual truth that transforms, enlightens, sanctifies. The church or the individual that is Bible taught without being Spirit taught (and there are many of them) has simply failed to see that truth lies deeper than the theological statement of it.[1]

Our information-laden, knowledgeable Christian society also bids us worship at the ancient, well-beloved shrine of knowledge and information—to our shame—and at great price. How naively we equate spiritual maturity with extensive knowledge. We may know a great deal about God without ever knowing God;

> know biblical content without living out biblical Christianity;
>
> know extensive passages of Scripture without ever integrating the truth contained therein into our individual lives.

John MacArthur clearly and succinctly summarizes the danger inherent in the worship of this idol: *"Spiritual growth has nothing to do with knowledge.* A person may have a lot of facts, a lot of information, but that can't be equated with spiritual maturity. Unless your knowledge results in conforming you to Christ, it is useless. It must be life-changing."[2]

It all comes down, then, to what we do with all our knowledge and information. It is their application to and

79 / Notebooks, Card Files, and Manila Folders

integration into our lives that is important. It is how we put our knowledge to use that is of value. Knowledge for knowledge's sake is worthless. Absolutely worthless. Exactly what good does it do for "sociologists to tell other sociologists?"

Or for Christians to tell other Christians?

Simply said, it is very easy to become lost in knowledge and information—totally lost.

> *So what about these wise men, these scholars, these brilliant debaters of this world's great affairs? God has made them all look foolish, and shown their wisdom to be useless nonsense. For God in his wisdom saw to it that the world would never find God through human brilliance, and then he stepped in and saved all those who believed his message, which the world calls foolish and silly. It seems foolish to the Jews because they want a sign from heaven as proof that what is preached is true; and it is foolish to the Gentiles because they believe only what agrees with their philosophy and seems wise to them. So when we preach about Christ dying to save them, the Jews are offended and the Gentiles say it's all nonsense. But God has opened the eyes of those called to salvation, both Jews and Gentiles, to see that Christ is the mighty power of God to save them; Christ himself is the center of God's wise plan for their salvation. This so-called "foolish" plan of God is far wiser than the wisest plan of the wisest man, and God in his weakness—Christ dying on the cross—is far stronger than any man.*
> 1 Corinthians 1:20–25 LB

Yes, it is *very easy* to become lost in knowledge and information.

> *When will you ever learn that "believing" is useless without doing what God wants you to? Faith that does not result in good deeds is not real faith.*
> *Don't you remember that even our father Abraham was*

> *declared good because of what he* did, *when he was willing to obey God, even if it meant offering his son Isaac to die on the altar? You see, he was trusting God so much that he was willing to do whatever God told him to; his faith was made complete by what he did, by his actions, his good deeds....*
>
> *Just as the body is dead when there is no spirit in it, so faith is dead if it is not the kind that results in good deeds.*
>
> James 2:20–22, 26 LB

It is *very easy* to become *lost* in knowledge and information.

7 | "If Only I Had Enough"

One of the recent great blessings in my life has been the entrance into our home of my unofficially adopted daughter, now a primary-school teacher. During her student internship, and then as a substitute teacher awaiting permanent employment, she would frequently come home with some fascinating tale of what took place in the first or second grade that day. Often it was a rather remarkable commentary on contemporary society—played out on the stage of the early primary grades. Such was the experience she reiterated toward the end of her last school year at home.

The class of first and second graders with whom she was working as an instructional aide was to go on the annual end-of-the-school-year class picnic at a park in one of the adjoining communities. The teacher discussed extensively with the class in the days prior to the excursion plans for the day including the menu to be served. Typically, the children chose all the usual picnic and cookout fare: hamburgers, hot dogs, fruit punch, watermelon, and ice cream. All the children were included in the decision-making; all were pleased with the selection of food. Great anticipation followed and the day chosen for the outing was all sunshine and blue sky. It would be a great day!

As might be expected, the school bus was a noisy conglomeration of happy chatter, boisterous laughter, and gaily sung songs. Obviously everyone was in a mood of happy anticipation, and a delightful feeling of class unity pervaded the atmosphere. Unfortunately such a feeling soon disappeared, for shortly after arrival at the park the class divided itself into two distinct segments—those who had spending money and those who had none.

The teacher of the class had quite casually mentioned a "picnic store" to the children some days prior to the outing, and for several of the children the highlight of the day seemed to be spending as much money as possible. Although the adults had provided food in abundance—the selection of which was made by the children, you will recall—three or four of the class members began almost immediately to haunt the small concession stand. One little girl in particular seemed to stand out in her purchasing power. She had brought with her a total of five dollars (rather remarkable in itself for a seven-year-old's half day at the park) and seemed intent upon spending as much of it as possible. First, she purchased a soft drink, then a box of popcorn (I think I would have reversed the order) followed by a large, "all day" sucker. All eyes were upon her.

Just as the class-selected picnic fare was not adequate for this child, the one train ride on which all of the class had gone was also insufficient; *she* went on an *additional* ride. It was not long before this young lady was elevated to the status of folk-hero in the eyes of her classmates. Money talks, and these children were hearing its powerful voice! One child was even seen wandering among the picnic tables aimlessly muttering, "If only I had a nickel!" When asked, "Why?" her response was simply, "Then I could buy something."

Something.

Anything.

The finale of this little story came after lunch when the teacher brought forth the cups of vanilla and chocolate ice cream. "Ooh"s and "Aah"s were followed by simple, silent enjoyment. Nothing is quite as delightful to a young child as that cool, creamy, delectable confection on a hot summery day! Nothing, that is, until something seemingly more satisfying comes into view; for sure enough, our heroine sauntered down from the picnic store, soft-serve cone in hand. Suddenly all eyes were riveted on the young lady with the money and the *cone* in her hand. Enjoyment of the half-eaten cups of ice cream was reduced to disappointment as the children cried out, "Where'd you get *that?*" And instead of "Thanks for the ice cream, Miss K," the only remark heard was, "If only I had enough. . . ."

"If only I had enough"—a rather remarkable commentary on contemporary society, played out in the lives of six- and seven-year-old children. Our whining, covetous, discontented worship at the idol of materialism and the good life presents itself.

Possibly no other false god is more personal, gets closer to the heart of each of us, or allures us so insidiously and cunningly as does this one. The captivating and enticing seduction of comfort, pleasure, and wealth—to say nothing of our personal ease, contentment, and indulgence—is very difficult to resist—and few of us do.

This idol of materialism and the good life holds such a prominent place in our society that it is constantly and clearly presented to us and cleverly promoted for our consideration. One might say that there is a shrine on every corner; or that every time we turn around, we encounter an invitation to worship. Those most committed to and interested in what has been called by some the American economic system, are the most devout proselytizers. Advertisers and marketing executives have persuaded most of us to believe that they know what we need, that they know better than we what constitutes the good life, that they have the answer to humanity's contentment. As if we know no other way, we who name the name of Christ fall prey to this Madison-Avenue hype. We heed the enticing pronouncements of what we must have to be happy and content, and join our non-Christian counterparts in the all-pervading tendency to be far more concerned with material than with spiritual values or goals. The doctrine of materialism (did you know that the dictionary defines materialism as a doctrine?) has been so effectively promoted that all of us have succumbed at one time or another, if not consistently, to its worship. Perhaps this idol, above all others, is the great competitor for our affection and esteem. Nor should this surprise us. Note what the Word says.

> *People will be lovers of themselves, lovers of money, boastful, proud, abusive, disobedient to their parents, ungrateful, unholy . . . without self-control . . . lovers of pleasure rather than lovers of God—having a form of godliness but denying its power.* 2 Timothy 3:2–5

How easy it has been for the entrepreneurs to play upon our self-centeredness and self-absorption! Our society promotes a spirit of hedonism as perhaps no other ever has, and with our propensity for self-indulgence facilitating their task, marketing experts have convinced us that ease, comfort, pleasure, and entertainment are the basics of what constitutes the good life.

Lovers of pleasure rather than lovers of God . . .
having a form of godliness but denying its power. . . .
Thus do we sigh and whisper a resigned "amen" accompanied by, "If only I had enough. . . ."

If only I had enough.
>   For what, exactly?
> Basic necessities of life?
>> Or the latest promoter's enticement?

Whatever the reason, whether it is the influence of Madison Avenue or that of our neighbors, business colleagues or family friends, we deny God's power to make a real difference in our everyday lives. Thus we find ourselves conforming to the world around us (how intertwined are all the idols!) by becoming absorbed by the necessity to own things. Nor does it seem to matter a great deal exactly what it is that we possess as long as it is what everyone else also has (or at least would like to have). We purchase items we do not need, frequently with money we do not have. Then, because we have purchased them at such great price, we spend much of our time in using and caring for them, to say nothing of the months—or even years—it takes to finish paying for them. We jump on almost any bandwagon if it has been effectively marketed—

> collecting items we really think are junk but have been told are valuable;
>> engaging in activities that often bore us but keep us fashionable and amused;
>>> purchasing conveniences we cannot afford but that give us comfort and ease.

Somehow we have confused our wants with our needs and, no longer being able to discern between the two, we have become caught up in simply acquiring things because we want them. Should we wonder, then, that our children do likewise?

In some homes, all this acquiring can cause a problem. Room after room becomes cluttered, and the latest device on the market cannot be purchased because there is no room for it. Neither is there space in the closet, or dresser drawer, or garage, or family room, or kitchen, or whatever—for the most recently advertised item to be housed *there*. What to do?

To forgo the acquisition of what we *want* is surely not the answer.

In my area of the country, instead of giving items to the Goodwill or to the Salvation Army (whose donations are down significantly), the solution to such a problem is found in the very popular "tag sale," several of which can be found in operation on any given weekend. Although some may defend such sales as the means by which one can purchase good, used items for much less money (and I would basically agree since few items show significant wear), I see them also—and primarily—as a convenient means of getting rid of outdated models and styles in order to facilitate the purchase of new equipment, clothing, and gadgets. One has only to visit some of these sales to see what is meant here. Although many are appealing to the compulsive buying syndrome displayed in our society by offering the latest in "collectibles" (and there are now books available describing currently sought-after items), many of these home sales are filled with good, serviceable, "like new" items that are simply outdated. Space as well as money is needed in order to acquire
 the newer,
   more convenient,
      more up-to-date,
         more fashionable

piece of equipment, article of clothing, appliance, gadget, or toy. Built-in obsolescence is a fact of life; few there are who seem capable of withstanding its resultant allure for the "new and better." Thus our homes are filled—filled with every possible contrivance for
> our ease,
>> our comfort,
>>> our convenience.

They are replete with things. Mostly new things.

Let us be careful; our avarice is showing. We are whining, covetous, discontented worshipers at the idol of materialism and the good life.

Nowhere is this seen more clearly than in our leisure pursuits and acquisitions. As a matter of fact, it may well be in our leisure that we are the most conspicuous in our self-centeredness and self-indulgence. In our highly individual-oriented society, family members must have their own personal television sets (it is not at all uncommon to find four or five sets in one home), stereo equipment, cassette players, latest model cameras, and most recently promoted video games.

The newest entrance into the classification of "necessities" is the personal computer, currently being promoted by the electronics industry via summer computer camps for children (they know the market toward which to aim!). Thousands of youth are attending such camps, while more traditional resident summer camps seem to be experiencing a decline in attendance. Additional young people are enrolled in day clinics designed to introduce them to the delights and dilemmas of computer manipulation and problem solving. In contemporary America, addiction equals need, and as *Newsweek* observes; "Many campers become computer addicts. One instructor at Texas Instruments, which operates day sessions at YMCA's and schools in

24 cities, predicts that 75 percent of those attending the ten-hour courses will have new personal computers at home within a week—and the company expects as many as 50,000 kids to enroll in the program this year."[1] This is just what the marketing experts had hoped. Make no mistake, home video disc players and video games are the stepping stones to personal computers, and families are eagerly rushing to buy this newest toy.

The computer is not the culprit, however; the real culprit is our insistence upon having whatever is currently marketed and promoted. Although video games and personal computers lead, in my opinion, to further individualization, self-absorption, and isolation, they are not the real issues. The point of concern is that we are simply sold out to—enslaved by—the idea that we must have what we want, or what we have been persuaded we want. Regardless.

Regardless meaning that we will forfeit precious *time*—time with our family or our friends or our Lord—in order to work and acquire more financial assets to enable us to purchase more "necessities."

Regardless meaning that we will allow ourselves to be duped into thinking that the more costly, exotic, and exciting an experience is, the better it must be—though we are often met with disappointment.

Regardless meaning that we will run from one costly activity to another, purchasing newer, better equipment and attire because someone has convinced us that the equipment and the clothing will "make all the difference."

Regardless that it can be said that we are "lovers of themselves . . . lovers of money . . . ungrateful . . . without self-control . . . lovers of pleasure rather than lovers of God."

Regardless.

Confusing our wants with our needs often leads to great dissatisfaction and a lack of contentment, resulting in a striving for more and more. Nor should this surprise us. The Word says,

> *But godliness with contentment is great gain. For we brought nothing into the world, and we can take nothing out of it. But if we have food and clothing, we will be content with that. People who want to get rich fall into temptation and a trap and into many foolish and harmful desires that plunge men into ruin and destruction. For the love of money is a root of all kinds of evil. Some people, eager for money, have wandered from the faith and pierced themselves with many griefs.*
>
> 1 Timothy 6:6–10

Indeed, we have pierced *ourselves* with our whining, covetous, discontented worship at the idol of materialism and the good life.

In our pursuit of the good life, we are pursued.
In our consumption, we are, ourselves, consumed.

When will we ever have enough of—"If only I had enough"?

Seventy years are given us! And some may even live to eighty. But even the best of these years are often emptiness and pain; soon they disappear, and we are gone.

Teach us to number our days and recognize how few they are; help us to spend them as we should.

Psalm 90:10, 12 LB

8 | "His Yoke Is Easy, His Burden Light"

Since entering the field of leisure studies, I have come to view introductions to strangers with mixed emotions. It is not that I don't enjoy meeting new people. As a matter of fact, I really *like* people, but it is all those introductory topics of conversation that bother me. For example: how would *you* like it if, upon hearing the field of endeavor to which you have given your undivided professional attention, the person with whom you are becoming acquainted says, "Oh. *That* sounds like fun. What do you do—teach people how to watch TV?" At this juncture there are usually gales of laughter, followed by a rather awkward silence.

Of course my new acquaintance knows that I don't really teach people how to view TV and, sensing my discombobulation, ventures, "What, exactly, do you teach? I've never heard of an academic program in *leisure*. I can't imagine what you *do!*" and the social intercourse begins. When I have explained that we study the phenomenon of leisure, its impact upon society, the economy and the quality of life, and that we then endeavor to assist individuals in finding meaning in their leisure, the next phase begins.

If my new friend is male, he will adjust his tie—or smooth his hair if he has no tie—or hitch up his trousers if he has no hair. If my acquaintance is female, she will adjust her skirt—or her glasses—or smooth out the non-existent wrinkles in her skirt or slacks. Both will sit up just a bit straighter or somehow stand taller. Both will also inevitably place a hand to the chin and, with a slight tilt of the head and a condescending air, proclaim, "I *have* no leisure." I can't tell you how many people have told me this. Nor can I believe how many individuals appear to be really *proud* of the fact that they seem to have no free time.

Be honest now. What is *your* response to the idea of an abundance of free time?

Or of any free time at all?

Could it possibly be that you, too, are among the multitudes who worship at the altar of
work,
productivity,
accomplishment?

Is it conceivable that you, too, are among the myriad of individuals who, knowing that there *must* be more to life than is currently experienced, are searching for—hoping for—
a depth of satisfaction heretofore unknown,
a meaning and purpose for human existence not yet experienced,
a respite from the rat race found in contemporary society?

Of all people, Christians should know the real meaning and purpose of life, yet we conduct ourselves as if we were

"His Yoke Is Easy, His Burden Light"

on the same, identical merry-go-round of existence as our non-believing friends, grasping at the brass rings of
    crowded schedules,
        filled-up calendars,
            busy days and busy lives.

We purport to have found satisfaction in our personal relationship with the Redeemer King, yet we live as spiritual paupers, bereft of peace and tranquility in our daily lives, striving—working at everything—to illustrate our worth.

We must produce,
    we must accomplish,
        we must be busy.
            But *why?*

Why, indeed, when *Jesus* said,

> *Come to me, all you who are weary and burdened, and I will give you rest. Take my yoke upon you and learn from me, for I am gentle and humble in heart, and you will find rest for your souls. For my yoke is easy and my burden is light.*
>
> Matthew 11:28–30

I suggest that many of us as Christians know very little about this rest for our souls. We are too busy in the conduct of our lives—in our ministries, if you would—to be even aware of the state of our souls! Jesus invites us to *learn* from Him; but where is the gentleness, the humbleness of heart of which our Lord spoke? Do you honestly believe that rest, gentleness, and humility are expressed in our frenetic lifestyles?

What is it about our lives that makes us the salt of the earth, the light of the world?

Just how different are we from our non-Christian neighbors, business colleagues, fellow students?

Indeed, just how different *are* we?

Perhaps the Amplified version of the above passage will broaden our understanding of just how radical a difference Jesus *can* make in our lives—if we will but allow Him.

> *Come to Me, all you who labor and are heavy-laden and overburdened, and I will cause you to rest — I will ease and relieve and refresh your souls.*
>
> *Take My yoke upon you, and learn of Me; for I am gentle (meek) and humble (lowly) in heart, and you will find rest — relief, ease and refreshment and recreation and blessed quiet — for your souls.*
>
> *For My yoke is wholesome (useful, good) — not harsh, hard, sharp or pressing, but comfortable, gracious and pleasant; and My burden is light and easy to be borne.*

If Jesus' yoke is truly easy and His burden light, then why do we bend beneath them so? Why do we insist upon encumbering ourselves with the fetters of constant productivity and accomplishment, carrying these shackles with us even into our leisure? Why do we act as if we must *pursue* the abundant life when it is provided for us in Christ Jesus? Why are there so few of us who know what it means to truly rest on the bosom of the Father in quietness and trust? Why do so few non-believers view the Christian life as little different from their own?

Why?

Could it be that in all reality we are little different from our non-Christian counterparts?

As an assist in thinking about all this, let's return to chapter 2 for a moment and review what it is we're talking about when we speak of leisure. There we defined leisure as the period of time in an individual's daily life that is devoted neither to existence nor subsistence needs, and that, therefore, may be considered unobligated or discretionary time. It implies an attitude of freedom, especially freedom of choice.

If anyone should comprehend freedom, it is the

"His Yoke Is Easy, His Burden Light"

Christian, for the Christian alone is truly free. Yet few of us are living out our freedom in Christ. Rather, we are demonstrating to the world about us that we are as enslaved to the world and its idols as is the non-believer. We seem to understand little about being a bond slave to Christ, substituting the freedom involved in this relationship (something of a paradox) for bondage to false gods.

Few Christians are any different at all from their non-Christian friends in their devotion to the idols of
> conformity and appearance,
>> success and achievement,
>>> knowledge and information,
>>>> materialism and the good life.
>>>>> *Our lifestyles confirm this.*

Lifestyle, as you will recall, is the manner in which we conduct our lives, based upon our value system and reflecting those values in the management of our resources, the expenditure of our time and energy, and the establishment of our relationships. It is the clear, distinctive expression of what we hold dear.

We must ask ourselves, then, if the manner in which we conduct our lives is at all different—to say nothing of its being radically different—from our non-believing friends. This dissimilarity must be in the everyday of life; in the things we choose to
> do, say, engage in,
>> purchase, neglect, pursue,
>>> read, experience, view.

In the things we *choose* to
> do, say, engage in,
>> purchase, neglect, pursue,
>>> read, experience, view.

Precisely how do our values differ from those about us, as *expressed in our lifestyles?*

Since it is in our leisure that we make the most choices pertaining to our lifestyles, for those things involving our existence and subsistence needs are reasonably fixed (though not, of course, without *any* choices), it behooves us to take a long, hard look at our leisure lifestyles.

Most of us fall into one of two patterns in our leisure. First, and perhaps most typical, are those of us who fear the empty hours of our increasing free time; thus we fill them. Nor does it matter a great deal with what we fill these hours as long as they are somehow without void. Consequently we run from
> meeting to meeting,
> > entertainment to entertainment,
> > > activity to activity.

We run from one project to another, making sure we have no quiet moments, no time without some involvement. We do *anything* to fill our time.

Although many of our activities are in and of themselves commendable (though many indeed are not!), why is it that we find it so difficult to spend time with ourselves, with our Lord, in quiet contemplation? Why are the times so rare that we spend with our families or our friends, giving them our full attention and getting to know them in the everyday of life—and letting them know us?

Overinvolvement,
> endless activity,
> > passive amusement and entertainment

lead to such isolation from one another, and few of us are even aware that it could be otherwise. Whoever said that all motion is easier than quiet contemplation was absolutely right. To be busy is so much easier than to be quiet; to be involved with things is so much more simple than to be involved, truly involved, with the people we love.

Thus we busy ourselves with a variety of rather meaningless amusements, frequently being caught in the trap (some call it neurosis) of consumerism. We purchase items, activities, and experiences that we think will bring us satisfaction in our leisure, only to discover that the latest acquisition or involvement is as disappointing as the last. Not only must we contend with the planned obsolescence in our purchases, but with the unplanned boredom and ennui brought about by our being saturated with goods and services. We consume our time with the consumption of things and find ourselves used up as well.

If you find yourself caught up in what the marketing experts advise is the most recent answer to life's humdrumities, I suggest that some things need to be rethought, and values reassessed.

The second leisure lifestyle belongs to the people who say, "I *have* no leisure," and to those who look upon the whole idea of free time—any free time—with disdain. This we could term the "no leisure" lifestyle wherein we measure the value of our lives, as well as our leisure, totally on the basis of work values. We carry over into our leisure the drives for accomplishment and productivity, working both *in* our leisure and *at* our leisure pursuits, thus robbing ourselves of the unique contributions they could make to our lives. As a result, our leisure hours are filled with more work-oriented experiences—sometimes with work itself—either moonlighting or bringing work home. The

workaholics found worshiping at the throne of success and achievement are often also found here, totally ignoring even the idea of leisure. How many individuals do you know whose entire sense of worth, whose entire lives are so involved in productivity and accomplishment—even in their leisure—that they
> know their families not at all,
>> spend little time alone with God,
>>> are overcommitted, overworked, and
>>>> overwrought?

Frequently this drive for productivity and accomplishment in the Christian is seen in the near compulsion to be involved in "the Lord's work"—to the point that Christian activity (and I use that term advisedly) becomes an all-consuming passion. There are many of us Christians who think of ourselves as less than we should be (whatever that is) if we do not accept any and every invitation to be involved in "Christian service." Why should we think that a need for someone to be involved in a given area of ministry means we are automatically called to this service? I remind you of a deeply penetrating truth shared with me by a friend: the *need* does *not* constitute the *call*.

Often Christians say that if you want anything done, ask the busy person. What a travesty of Christian commitment! It is better to reevaluate the worth of the task itself than to further contribute to the overcommitment of individuals who are already neglecting themselves, their families and friends, and their Lord! How much better to pray and wait for God's Spirit to appoint the person of His choosing than to settle for an already overworked individual. When we are so involved—even in the Lord's work—that our lives are hectic, rushed, and breathless, and there is little time for quiet communion with the Source of all strength and power, we are too involved.

Some radical steps must be taken by Christians if we are to begin to make an impact upon our society. What is called for, I believe, is a basic change in lifestyle, providing for quality leisure experiences. This fundamental change in the manner in which we conduct ourselves in our leisure is imperative, for we cannot introduce people to what we do not have ourselves. Life begets life just as faith kindles faith; we cannot give what we do not possess.

We cannot offer—or even suggest—rest to others when we know no genuine rest ourselves.

We cannot present the abundant life if we know little or nothing of its real meaning in our own lives.

We cannot lead others to the true God while we continue our worship of man-made gods.

We cannot introduce others to the living, loving Savior if we have no meaningful, dynamic relationship with Him.

We cannot suggest that others change until we change ourselves.

9 | A Unique Opportunity

I was on a flight to Chicago, where several professional commitments awaited me. I had purposely chosen a window seat so I could look out into space and be alone with my thoughts, for I was preoccupied. What an understatement! I had just placed my mother in the hospital—stopping to do so en route to the airport; the awaiting responsibilities were significant. Mother's condition, although not life-threatening, was serious; I had taught two classes at the university before the rather involved departure, and I was weary. The *last* thing I wanted to do was to talk with some stranger on a plane. Surely to sit raptly gazing out the window would ward off anyone.

Not so!

The plane was filled to capacity, and the frequently empty middle seat was soon occupied. I didn't look up to acknowledge anyone's presence, but it was not long before a deep masculine voice interrupted my reverie with, "Pardon me, how far are you going?" I turned to find a very young (and very handsome!) naval officer sitting beside me, obviously wanting someone with whom to talk. Apparently he decided forty and graying was to be preferred over sixty-five and bald, and it wasn't long before we were engaged in conversation.

As is usually the case, the topic of vocation arose and we were soon off and running on the leisure track. Surprisingly enough, this young man didn't find my occupation quite so unbelievable as most and he seemed intensely interested in what it was all about. When I told him that I had taught a class just that morning, he inquired about the content of the day's lecture. Could I—would I—please give it to him in a nutshell?

To ask a college professor to give much of anything in a nutshell is a brave request indeed, but since he asked, I tried. One of the statements I had made that morning was something I had read somewhere by Charles Brightbill: "Tell me what you do in your leisure—when you are free to do just as you please—and I'll tell you the kind of person you are."

Although I had used that statement endless times and in a variety of situations, I had often wondered just how one might go about proving its validity. I had never really attempted to identify the sort of person someone might be by analyzing his—or her—leisure pursuits, but I had supposed it could be readily done if Charlie Brightbill had found it so. Now I suddenly found myself in a situation where I might, indeed, prove (or disprove!) the validity of the statement, for my new friend, jumping upon the opportunity to have an "expert" tell him about himself, exclaimed, "Let's do it! I'll tell you about all the things I do in my free time and you tell me the kind of person I am."

I nearly fainted. This young naval officer was challenging me to prove what I didn't really *know* could be proven! Thus our experiment began. It wasn't long before we were engaged in an enlightening conversation, with my seatmate describing his varied leisure pursuits and my evaluating them with him, pointing out various apparent character traits. It really worked! I can't recall all the details now (twelve years later), but he was totally amazed (to say nothing of how astonished I was) that an absolute stranger could discover so much about him and his life's purpose simply through a truthful recounting of his leisure involvements. It was true: what he did in his leisure—when he was free to do just as he pleased—clearly revealed the kind of individual he was. And the same holds true for each of us.

So tell me—what do *you* do in your leisure—when you are free to do just as you please?
Do you fill it with meaningless activity?
Do you deny its very existence?
Or do you embrace it as the unique opportunity it is?
For it *is* an opportunity, you know—a tremendous opportunity.

First, and maybe foremost, leisure is the opportunity to place greater emphasis on making a *life* than on making a *living*.[1] I will never forget the first time I read a sentence similar to that and the impact it had upon my thinking. It is absolutely true: Leisure—discretionary time—is a unique opportunity for making a *life*. It is the occasion for setting aside our existence and subsistence interests, activities, and responsibilities and emphasizing life—or, if you would, relationships.

Relationships, if I read God's Word correctly, are the essence of life. Throughout Scripture God points us to the need for, establishment, and development of relationships. As illustrated first in Genesis when the Lord said, "It isn't good for man to be alone; I will make a companion for him, a

helper suited to his needs" (Genesis 2:18 LB), the theme of relationships is developed throughout the whole of Scripture.
 Faithfulness, trust, honesty;
  loyalty, purity, devotion;
   forgiveness, graciousness, mercy;
    all are there.
Consistently throughout the unfolding of the Word there is great detail given concerning the relationships of individuals to one another as well as to the Lord God. And we see the climax of it all when God's only Son is sent to earth from the very throne of heaven to provide the means for establishing personal relationship with human beings! Since the Word clearly addresses the area of relationships, we must search the Scriptures for guidelines pertaining to our methods of relating to people—and then follow those guidelines.

Leisure is the opportunity to become truly acquainted with loved ones, to enjoy one another, to share hopes and dreams, hurts and disappointments, happy, fun times and times of distress. Leisure is the opportunity to play with our children, to nurture and enjoy them; it is the occasion to open ourselves to our mates and to listen—really listen—to them and hear what they are saying. How well do we know the people with whom we share our lives? How well do they know us?

Leisure also gives us the opportunity to reach out to build relationships outside our families, and to allow others to reach out to us. I am convinced, as a counselor myself, that *many* individuals who are now seeing counselors and therapists would have no need of such "purchased friendship" if leisure were used as the occasion to develop meaningful and lasting relationships. If, indeed, the essence of life is relationships, then where there are none of real significance there is little, if any, meaning to life. Is it any wonder so many of us find life rather meaningless and empty?

Speaking of meaningless and empty—perhaps it is also appropriate to ask how well we know ourselves. There are woefully few of us who spend any quiet moments in solitude and stillness, and we *must* ask, why? Is it because we are
afraid of what we will discover about ourselves?
uncomfortable with our own thoughts and feelings?
ashamed of the hollow, empty shells we have
become?
Are we so unacquainted with ourselves that we find it simply too painful and awkward to spend time alone with this someone we hardly know?

And speaking of someone we hardly know—perhaps it is now advisable to ask about the *depth* of our relationship with the Lord. Leisure provides the opportunity for meaningful communication with the people around us as well as the time for quiet meditation, soul-searching, and the occasional introspection we all need, but seldom pursue. Perhaps even more significantly, leisure is also that marvelously unique opportunity to be still—really still—before the Lord, to wait patiently for Him (Psalm 37:7), to know that He is God (Psalm 46:10). Again there are tragically few of us who withdraw into our closets, alone with God in quietness and rest, and we *must* ask, why? Is it because we are

107 / A Unique Opportunity

    afraid of what we will discover about Him?
        uncomfortable with His companionship alone, His thoughts?
            ashamed of the hollowness and emptiness of our lives before Him?

Are we so unacquainted with this One we purport to know and love that we find it simply too painful and too awkward to spend time alone with this someone we hardly know?

    Leisure is the opportunity to place greater emphasis on the things that *matter*.

    Leisure is also the opportunity to think in terms of our *total* persons. It is the occasion to bring our lives into balance. What a wonder we are as human beings created in the image of God! What varied dimensions there are in our lives. With David we can say, "You created me in my inmost being; you knit me together in my mother's womb. I praise you because I am fearfully and wonderfully made" (Psalm 139:13–14). Sometimes that thought simply overwhelms me! Fearfully and wonderfully made, indeed—with all the complexities of the physical, mental, social, and spiritual dimensions of our beings. There are so many aspects to our lives, yet each of us is surely greater than the mere sum of our parts.

    Have you ever thought of how little we know about the Lord Jesus as a young child, as an adolescent, as a young adult? I have. And though there are many things that we might like to know about the Messiah's early years, somehow God didn't think it was necessary for us to be apprised of the details of His earthly life until the time He began His ministry. However, in His sovereignty, God did deign to disclose to us the developmental pattern of Christ's life as revealed in Luke 2:52: "And Jesus grew in wisdom and stature, and in favor with God and men."

>Jesus grew (matured)
>>in wisdom (intellectually)
>>>in stature (physically)
>>>>in favor with God (spiritually)
>>>>>in favor with men (socially).

Whatever we might not know about the Lord's earthly life, this we do know: Jesus was a total person; He matured in every dimension of His life. The Word says that He was the perfectly balanced individual. He was no one-sided eccentric. He knew no excesses of any kind. He was neither faddist nor fanatic. Jesus was a *balanced* person.

Though none of us will ever have our lives in perfect balance, for perfection belongs to God alone, doesn't it behoove us as Christians to follow the example of the Master? Leisure is the opportunity to bring our lives into this balance He illustrates.

Though many of us perceive this balance as something attained by compensation, this is not what is meant here. It is, of course, true that if we use our bodies more than our minds in our subsistence endeavors, our leisure pursuits can tax and tease our intellects; or if we lead sedentary work lives, our leisure can assist us in bringing the physical dimension of our lives into balance. It is also true that if our work requires much interpersonal involvement, our leisure can offer us the opportunity for quiet and solitude; and whatever our work and its ensuing demands and responsibilities, our leisure provides for the "coming apart with our Lord" that we all need if we are to grow and mature spiritually.

The balance of which we speak here, however, is not simply the use of our leisure pursuits as compensation for

what is missing in our work, but it is our view of leisure itself as the unique opportunity for bringing balance into the *whole* of our lives. Leisure is the opportunity
> to emphasize the totality, the entirety, the integrity of our lives;
>> to recognize that we are composite beings, not just breadwinners, homemakers, students or Christian workers;
>>> to maximize the inherited characteristics of God, in whose image we are created.

Leisure is the opportunity to
> express our creativity,
>> exercise our talents,
>>> examine the world around us,
>>>> exert our bodies in physical activity,
>>>>> exchange ideas with a friend,
>>>>> expand our interests,
>>>>> expel our boredom,
>>>>> exult in God!

Conclusions must be reached individually. Each person's balance will be unique. But we do *need* this balance if we are to live out meaningful lives.

There is no simple formula to follow, but should you wonder just how to make decisions regarding balancing your life in your leisure, I offer the following diagram, developed by Jay B. Nash, one of the earliest American recreation and leisure philosophers, for your consideration. Perhaps it will be helpful as you consider your own leisure lifestyle. Nash contends that we all need some involvement in each of the positive areas identified in the pyramid. Needless to say, those leisure pursuits in the negative area are to be avoided,

MAN'S USE OF LEISURE

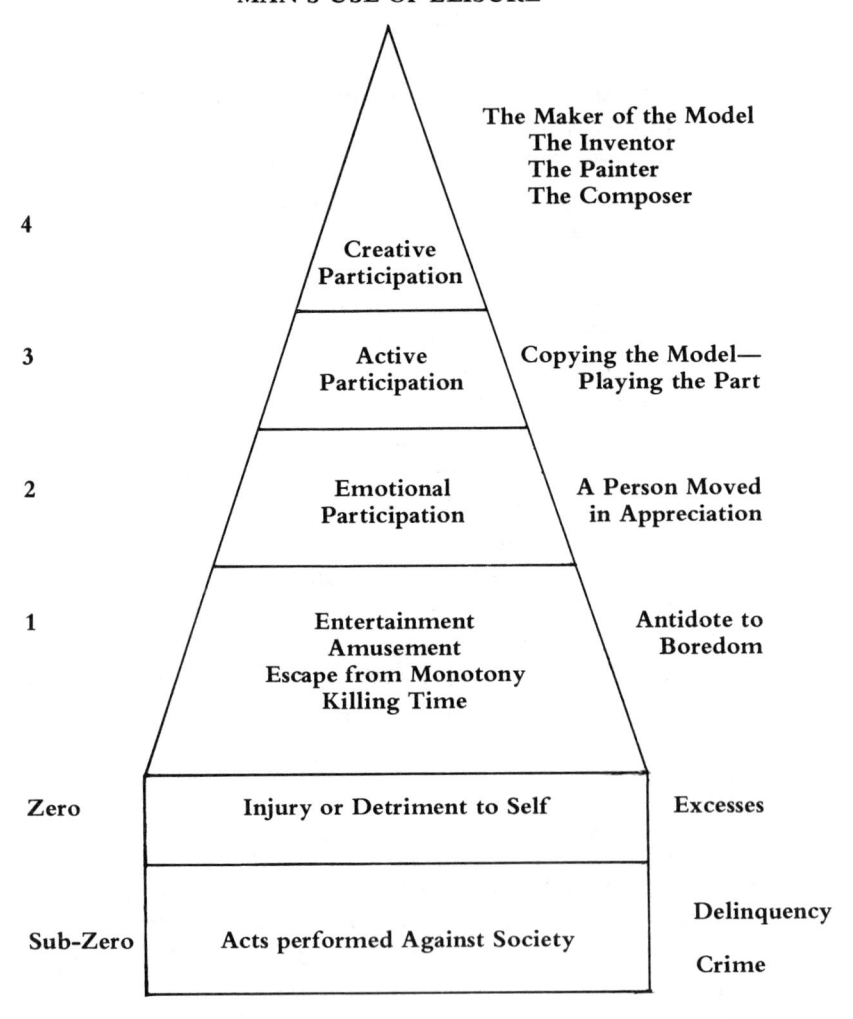

4	Creative Participation	The Maker of the Model The Inventor The Painter The Composer
3	Active Participation	Copying the Model— Playing the Part
2	Emotional Participation	A Person Moved in Appreciation
1	Entertainment Amusement Escape from Monotony Killing Time	Antidote to Boredom
Zero	Injury or Detriment to Self	Excesses
Sub-Zero	Acts performed Against Society	Delinquency Crime

Jay B. Nash[2]

and we are well-advised to note that *anything* in excess results in injury or detriment to self. Even the "plus" areas of pursuits can very easily be carried to excess, becoming detrimental not only to self, but to family and friends as well.

If you were to categorize your leisure pursuits based upon Nash's pyramid, where would the majority of them fall? What does this suggest to you? I fear that far too many of us—Christian or not—if we are honest, would have to admit that many, if not most of our leisure involvements fall into the "Antidote to Boredom" category. We who claim to know the meaning and purpose of life seem not to know at all, and we are but passive spectators in the amusement and entertainment arena. Tozer, in *The Root of the Righteous,* says it so well:

> No one with common human feeling will object to the simple pleasures of life, nor to such harmless forms of entertainment as may help to relax the nerves and refresh the mind exhausted by toil. Such things if used with discretion may be a blessing along the way. That is one thing. The all-out devotion to entertainment as a *major activity* for which and by which men live is definitely something else again. The abuse of a harmless thing is the essence of sin.[3] (emphasis mine)

We *must* strive for balance and follow in obedience our Lord's example. What are you doing to enhance your life physically—mentally—socially—spiritually? What changes must be made in your leisure lifestyle to permit your *total* growth and development as an individual? What modifications must be made to make you the *whole* man or woman of God that He desires you to be? Leisure is the opportunity for establishing and maintaining balance in our lives.

Leisure is also the opportunity for enjoying the Creator and the wonder of His works, yet all too frequently we are so involved in filling our discretionary time with the "plastics" of life that we completely overlook the substance of God's creation about us.

>Sunsets, violets, a blade of grass,
>>children at play, a rippling stream,
>>>fragrance of damp leaves,
>>>>morning mist, dew-drenched rose, star-filled sky,

all slip by us in the rush and breathlessness of our busy days and busy lives.

These and a myriad of other wonders of God's marvelous creation stand waiting for our enjoyment, and as we respond to their bidding we discover that He—Creator, Sustainer of all that is, was or ever will be—also stands waiting, waiting for our enjoyment of Him, the One who designed and made it all. Such is the way of this wondrous Lord we dare to call our own.

It has been my custom for several years to go away for a few days each spring and fall on a sort of solo retreat. Whenever possible, I head for the coast of Maine and spend my solitary time on the rocks at ocean's edge. I sometimes think the manager of the motel in which I stay dreads to see me come, for nearly every time I stay at Bald Head Cliff (my favorite spot) there is a ferocious storm—always just for me, I am convinced.

I love to watch it brew, filling sky and sea with dark, foreboding clouds, and deep ocean swells. Cool breezes become sharp, chilling winds; the gentle mist blowing off the water becomes a driving rain. Crash of waves upon the rocks blends with the loud claps of thunder, and the sky is punctuated with the gigantic fireworks display, sometimes known as lightning. God's handiwork is manifest just for my enjoyment!

Once the lightning has disappeared and danger is abated, I don my yellow rubber boots and well-worn rain suit and head out into the wind and rain. What an absolutely marvelous experience! Water beating against my face, wind against my body, totally *aware* of the elements, I am also *totally aware* of my Lord. Psalms of praise fall from my lips, and loud are the hymns of adoration flung across the sky from the depths of my heart! My leisure has afforded me the opportunity to *enjoy* my Lord in the midst of His creation!

Nor is it only in the ferocity of storms that His handiwork is so visibly displayed, as this entry from my journal illustrates.

> I stood alone on the deck this evening, at twilight—and I looked—and my eyes drank in beauty and loveliness—found in the woodlands on an evening in springtime. I drew deep breaths and smelled things—and I closed my eyes and heard the evening noises speak to me—and I lowered my head in humbleness before my Lord—and spoke with Him of many things.
>
> But mostly I thanked Him—for Himself—for His life given for, and then to me—and for the *countless* blessings with which He has entrusted me.
>
> I also walked in solitude in the yard tonight—to feel the cool—and be enveloped in the darkness of the night—to gaze at the heavens and wonder at the stars—to see the black shapes silhouetted against the blue-black of the night sky, and to feel very small—to pause again in quietude and just *be*—with Jesus.
>
> Quiet, tender moments alone with Him.

Such experiences are not for a chosen few; they are available to any child of God. The beauty, the wonder, the majesty of creation is available for all. Leisure is the opportunity for enjoying the Creator and the wonder of His works.

Finally, leisure is the opportunity for discovering Life (with a capital L!) in Jesus Christ and for sharing it with others. Jesus said, "I have come that they may have life, and have it to the full" (John 10:10). What does that mean to you? Are you enjoying life to the full? Or are you, like so many others, equating the "abundant" life with the "good" life, confusing material possessions and busy social calendars with spiritual values and inner tranquility?

Not long ago a student came into my office, threw herself down onto the couch, and declared, "Doc, there is a terrible void in my life that I just can't fill. You seem to have found some answers that satisfy you; what are they?" How thankful I am that I had, indeed, found some answers.

She was a lovely young woman—bright, attractive, friendly and out-going. She had a host of friends, excellent grades, apparently enough money to feel comfortable, nice clothes, was in a good living situation. She had most everything we might associate with the good life.

But not the abundant life.

And she was wise enough to know it. She was living testimony of the truth in 1 John 5:11–12: "God has given us eternal life, and this life is in his son. He who has the Son has life; he who does not have the Son of God does not have life." She was lifeless.

She is not without life now. In that hour—in her leisure—she came face to face with the realization that without Christ she had no life. With Him she would have life abundant and forgiveness of sin; she would have a relationship with the triune God. She decided to commit her life to Jesus Christ.

Think back to the time that you entered into a personal relationship with Christ; was it not in your leisure? Most of the Christians I know met the Lord, not at their work, but in their free time—at church, over coffee or lunch with a friend, at a youth rally, in a children's weekday club, at summer camp, in a Bible study—or in some other leisure experience. Leisure is the opportunity for discovering Life in Jesus Christ.

Perhaps if you have not yet become personally acquainted with God through His Son, in your leisure you will discover the full meaning of the familiar Scripture verse from John's gospel, "For God so loved the world that he gave his one and only Son, that whoever believes in him shall not perish but have eternal life" (John 3:16). If you are now experiencing the eternal life of which this passage speaks, then leisure is the opportunity to share that Life with others. It is the occasion to develop relationships with the people around you (including your family!) and through those relationships to share the Lord you love.

As we use our leisure more wisely, as we become more balanced individuals, then we will have a Life to share with others. Leisure is a special opportunity for that sharing. But remember: we can't give away what we don't have.

Leisure is an opportunity—a tremendous opportunity. So tell me—what do *you* do in *your* leisure—when you are free to do just as you please?

No one can tell you exactly how to spend your leisure. There are several guidelines, however, to help you decide which leisure involvements to pursue. I share them with you here. Think about them, pray over them, and avail yourself of the opportunities inherent in God's wonderful gift of leisure.

> Do I enjoy it? Although it may not necessarily be *fun,* is it *enjoyable?* Do I engage in it because I like it or because someone has told me I should like it?
>
> Is it costly? Is it more than I can realistically afford? What will have to be sacrificed in order to experience or purchase it?
>
> *Precisely why* am I pursuing or purchasing the activity/equipment/clothing/experience? Is it merely a passing fad or trend?
>
> Is it flirting with the world? Am I coming as close as possible to the world, appearing as little different as possible?
>
> Does it contribute to a well-balanced life? (Refer to Nash's pyramid; check for excesses).
>
> How will it contribute to my *total* person, to the physical, mental, social, and spiritual dimensions of my life?
>
> Will it enhance relationships? With God, with family, with friends? Will it help me to know myself?
>
> Is it edifying? Will it lead to the growth and strength of my person?
>
> Is it compatible with the Holy Spirit dwelling within me? Is it something which would make Jesus happy?

Does it enhance my consciousness of God and contribute to godliness in my life?

So tell me—what do you do in your leisure—when you are free to do just as you please?

10 | Quantity Versus Quality

Time is a strange and wondrous thing, rarely seen, I fear, as the precious gift it is. We take it so for granted—time—and depending upon our circumstances, view it as

    time on our hands,

        hours to be filled

                or some elusive quantity that simply passes by.
How we take it for granted, spending it freely, occasionally even squandering it as if there were an inexhaustible supply awaiting our disposal.

    You mean there isn't?

    That's right.

    There isn't.

We would be wise to pray with the psalmist, "Teach us to number our days aright, that we may gain a heart of wisdom" (Psalm 90:12) as we ponder the truth contained in Ecclesiastes 3:11: "He has made everything beautiful in its time. He has set eternity in the hearts of men; yet they cannot fathom what God has done from beginning to end."

    Somehow, in the frenzied lifestyles of contemporary society, we have lost the vision of the great, eternal plan of

the Creator God, compressing our lives into the finite, the knowable. We who are admonished to make the best use of our time, to "live life, then, with a due sense of responsibility, not as men who do not know the meaning and purpose of life but as *those who do*" (Ephesians 5:15–16 PHILLIPS), pay little heed to such admonition and bend beneath the pressure to conform to the
    standards,
           ideals,
                  and philosophies of our valueless society.
We lack wisdom, nor do we seem to seek it, substituting instead
    knowledge,
        information,
           trivia.
Though God's plan is for beauty *in its time,* we rush headlong into almost everything—and anything—crowding out the Source of all things beautiful with
    synthetic,
        contrived
           imitations.
Though He has placed eternity in our hearts, we have succumbed to the idols we have made and that now surround us, and have cast aside His eternal Truth.

We pursue the good life rather than embrace the abundant life provided for us in Christ Jesus. We live in an age of entitlement, the era of right of ownership and immediate gratification, and we confuse our wants with our needs, becoming consumed by our own consumption.

    And we see time in terms of
      the clock,
          the calendar,
               the crowded schedules.

God has given us the marvelous gift of leisure, revealed in creation, and He invites us to use it, yet we remain stuck in the mire of work and productivity, attempting to prove our worth, somehow, and politely saying, "No, thank You" to God.

    "No, thank You"—to God!

        "No, thank You"—for the gift of leisure, that special kind of time.

    Special?
        Yes.
Because it is that time in which we are free
    to choose,
        to gain perspective,
            to bring our lives into balance,
                to find integration, wholeness, unity.
    Special?
        Yes.
Because it offers us such significant choices.

    It is a time to spend, squander, use up—or a time to invest wisely in the things that really matter.

    It is a time to fill with meaningless activity and amusement—or a time to find fulfillment in our Redeemer King.

    It is a time to lose ourselves in frenetic, frantic lifestyles—or a time to find ourselves and to discover Life in Jesus Christ.

    It is a time to vegetate in passivity and lack of challenge and stimulation—or a time to grow and develop into truly balanced individuals.

It is a time to simply *busy* ourselves—or a time to reflect, ponder and meditate, remembering that all motion is easier than quiet contemplation.

It is a time to add to the quantity of our lives—or a time to improve the quality of our lives.

What do you do in *your* leisure—when you are free to do just as you please?

Notes

PREFACE

[1] A. W. Tozer, *The Divine Conquest* (Harrisburg: Christian Publications, 1950), p. 11.

CHAPTER 1

[1] *New York Times,* June 18, 1981, pp. 1, 19, Sec. A.
[2] Lynn C. Landman, *Informing Social Change* (A Research Study; New York: The Alan Guttmacher Institute, 1980).
[3] Charles C. Brightbill, *The Challenge of Leisure* (Englewood Cliffs, N.J.: Prentice-Hall, 1960), p. 27.
[4] Ibid., p. 20.
[5] Richard Kraus, *Recreation and Leisure in Modern Society* 2nd ed. (Santa Monica: Goodyear Publishing, 1978), p. 9.
[6] Otto Friedrich, "The Robot Revolution," *Time,* December 8, 1980, p. 83.
[7] Ibid., pp. 76–77.
[8] Thomas M. Kando, *Leisure and Popular Culture in Transition* 2nd ed. (St. Louis: C. V. Mosby, 1980), p. 268, quoting Richard Kraus, *Recreation and Leisure in Modern Society* (New York: Appleton-Century-Crofts, 1971), pp. 141–42.)
[9] Reynold E. Carlson, Theodore R. Deppe, and Janet R. MacLean, *Recreation in American Life* (Belmont, Calif.: Wadsworth Publishing, 1963), pp. 3–4.

CHAPTER 2

[1] Kraus, *Recreation and Leisure,* p. 41.
[2] Ibid.

CHAPTER 3

¹Tozer, *The Divine Conquest*, p. 22.
²Rudolph F. Norden, *The Christian Encounters the New Leisure* (St. Louis: Concordia Publishing House, 1965), pp. 97–98.

CHAPTER 4

¹J. A. Walter, *Sacred Cows: Exploring Contemporary Idolatry* (Grand Rapids: Zondervan Publishing House, 1980), p. 14.
²Ibid.
³Ibid.
⁴"Bent—But Not Broken," *U. S. News and World Report*, June 16, 1980, pp. 48–49.
⁵Gary Clarke, "Flo, Sue Ellen, Alice: Taking a Closer Look at the Women We Watch on TV," *Family Circle*, May 19, 1981, pp. 12, 78–82.
⁶Gladys Dickelman, "The ERA Mystique: Schlock That Tastes Like Apple Pie," *Moody Monthly*, April 1982, p. 41.
⁷Ibid., p. 42.
⁸Francis A. Schaeffer, *A Christian Manifesto* (Westchester, Ill.: Crossway Books, 1981), p. 53.
⁹A. W. Tozer, *That Incredible Christian* (Harrisburgh: Christian Publications, 1964), p. 134.

CHAPTER 5

¹Frank Minirth, et al., *The Workaholic and His Family: An Inside Look* (Grand Rapids: Baker Book House, 1981), p. 28.
²Wayne Oates, *Confessions of a Workaholic* (New York: World Publishing, 1971), p. 6.
³Minirth, *The Workaholic*, p. 28.
⁴Oates, *Confessions*, p. 6.
⁵Minirth, *The Workaholic*, p. 15–16.
⁶James Dobson, M.D., *Hide or Seek* (Old Tappan, N.J.: Fleming H. Revell, 1974), p. 37–38.
⁷Tozer, *Incredible Christian*, p. 112.

CHAPTER 6

¹Tozer, *Incredible Christian*, pp. 92–94.
²John F. MacArthur, Jr., *Keys to Spiritual Growth* (Old Tappan, N.J.: Fleming H. Revell, 1976), p. 10.

CHAPTER 7

¹Susan Dentzer with David T. Friendly, "Computer Camps for Kids," *Newsweek*, July 19, 1982, p. 75.

CHAPTER 9

[1] Rudolph F. Norden, *The Christian Encounters the New Leisure* (St. Louis: Concordia Publishing House, 1965), p. 75.

[2] Jay B. Nash, *Philosophy of Recreation and Leisure* (Dubuque: Wm. C. Brown, 1960), p. 89.

[3] A. W. Tozer, *The Root of the Righteous* (Harrisburg: Christian Publications, 1955), pp. 31–32.

Suggested Reading

Brand, Paul, and Philip Yancey. *Fearfully and Wonderfully Made.* Grand Rapids: Zondervan Publishing House, 1980.

Brightbill, Charles. *The Challenge of Leisure.* Englewood Cliffs, N.J.: Prentice-Hall, 1960.

Hansel, Tim. *When I Relax I Feel Guilty.* Elgin, Ill.: David C. Cook, 1979.

Lehman, Harold D. *In Praise of Leisure.* Scottdale, Pa.: Herald Press, 1974.

Longacre, Doris Janzen. *Living More With Less.* Scottdale, Pa.: Herald Press, 1980.

Minirth, Frank, Paul Meier, Frank Wichern, Bill Brewer, and States Skipper, *The Workaholic and His Family: An Inside Look.* Grand Rapids: Baker Book House, 1981.

Norden, Rudolph F. *The Christian Encounters the New Leisure.* St. Louis: Concordia Publishing House, 1965.

Oates, Wayne. *Confessions of a Workaholic.* New York and Cleveland: World Publishing, 1971.

Packer, J. I. *Knowing God.* Downers Grove, Ill.: InterVarsity Press, 1973.

Tozer, A. W. *The Pursuit of God.* Harrisburg, Pa.: Christian Publications, 1948.

———. *The Divine Conquest.* Harrisburg: Christian Publications, 1950.

———. *The Knowledge of the Holy.* San Francisco: Harper & Row, 1961.

Walter, J. A. *Sacred Cows: Exploring Contemporary Idolatry.* Grand Rapids: Zondervan Publishing House, 1980.